BRICK
ANIMALS

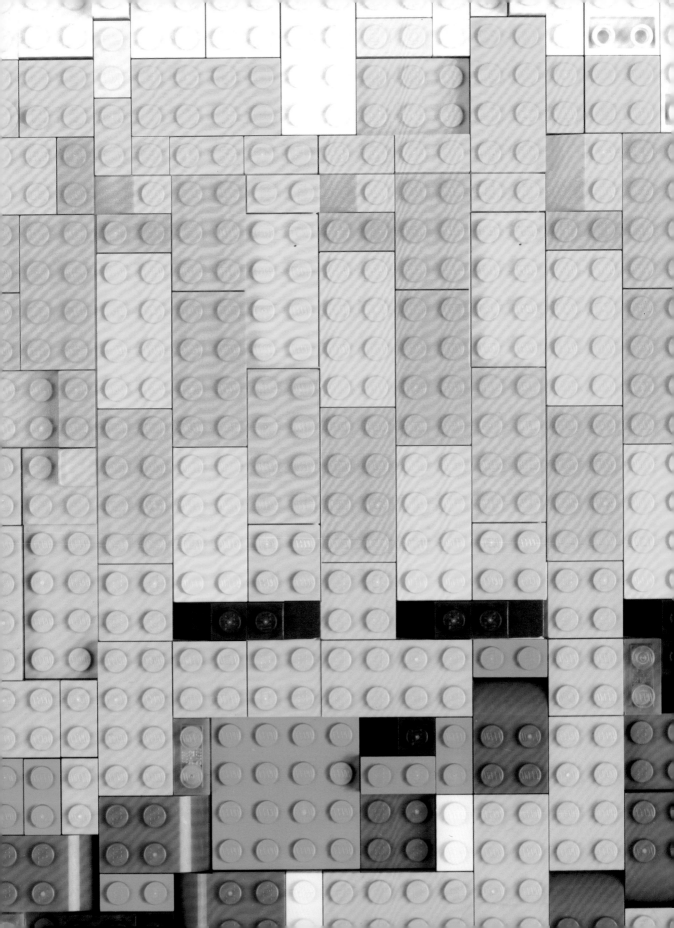

BRICK
ANIMALS

CLEVER AND CREATIVE IDEAS TO MAKE FROM CLASSIC LEGO®

WARREN ELSMORE

Buster Books

A Quintet Book

First published in Great Britain in 2016 by
Buster Books, an imprint of Michael O'Mara Books
Limited, 9 Lion Yard, Tremadoc Road,
London, SW4 7NQ

 www.busterbooks.co.uk

Buster Children's Books

@BusterBooks

ISBN 978-1-78055-446-4
QTT.BKITA

This book was conceived, designed and
produced by:
Quintet Publishing Limited
Ovest House
58 West Street
Brighton, East Sussex
BN3 1DD
United Kingdom

Photographer: Neal Grundy
Designer: Gareth Butterworth
Art Director: Michael Charles
Project Editor: Caroline Elliker
Editorial Director: Emma Bastow
Publisher: Mark Searle

10 9 8 7 6 5 4 3 2 1

Printed in China by C & C Offset Printing Co Ltd.

welcome to BRICK ANIMALS

When I work at public events building LEGO® models,
I'm often asked: 'Why does LEGO produce all these
special parts now? Back in my day it was all just bricks.'
Well, to prove that you can create anything from just
bricks, we decided to write this book.

The idea that The LEGO Company has changed its kit
and that specialist pieces are new isn't really correct.
Even back in 1950, when you could buy a box of basic
2 × 4 bricks, The LEGO Company still sold special
doors and windows! Wheels did take a little longer
to appear, but they have been a staple of any LEGO
model for 50 years now. So when we decided to build
a model out of 'basic bricks' we first had to decide
what a 'basic brick' was.

For this book, my team took their inspiration from the
LEGO CLASSIC sets. Each of these sets provides
exactly what those visitors I meet ask about: a big box
of LEGO bricks. Not every brick is a standard 2 × 4
brick, or 2 × 2 plate, or 1 × 3 slope – but everyone
should recognize the collection of LEGO pieces.

Colour is important for some of these animals,
although the coloured bricks available in the CLASSIC
boxes were not always the ones we wanted – that's
when having multiple CLASSIC boxes comes in handy!
When you're building these models yourself you can
change the colours according to the bricks you have
or the colour you want the animals to be.

Finally, if you want to build one of the models in this
book but don't have the right pieces – don't worry!
We spent lots of time trying to decide if we should
use one type of slope over another, but in the end it's
a personal decision. If your animal looks better with
a different piece, that's great! Remember, there is no
right or wrong with LEGO. As long as you've enjoyed
building the model, that's all that matters.

—Warren Elsmore

contents

Butterfly	6	Stork	50
Parrot	8	Lobster	52
Raccoon	10	Frog	54
Lion	13	Turkey	56
Rabbit	16	Shark	58
Duck	18	Horse	60
Beetle	20	Giraffe	63
Polar Bear	22	Camel	66
Fox	24	Swan	68
Elephant	27	Crab	70
Panda	30	Beaver	72
Seal	32	Antelope	75
Bumblebee	34	Warthog	78
Piranha	36	Mouse	80
Goat	38	Spider	82
Snake	40	Ant	84
Cat	42	Gorilla	86
Pig	44	Rhinoceros	88
Sheep	46	Flamingo	90
Cow	48	Mosquito	92
		Credits	96

butterfly

Building a butterfly in LEGO® is lots of fun, as they are very colourful creatures! For the rounded wing shape I used a combination of curved pieces and arches. The two arches give a nice form to the bottom of the wing and point it in the right direction. Curved slopes on the tops and sides of each wing round off the edges. I've used a 1 x 1 brick with studs to connect the wings.

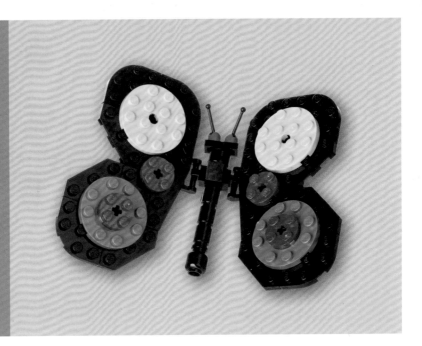

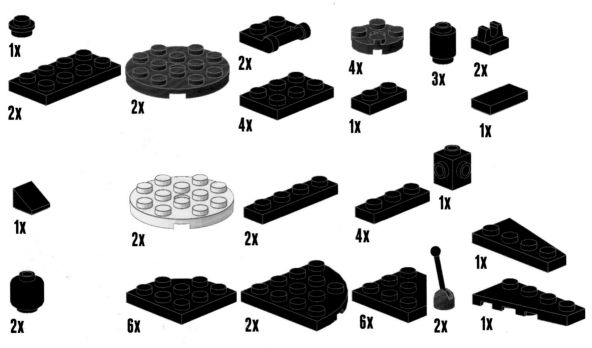

1x

2x

2x

2x

4x

2x

4x

1x

4x

3x

2x

1x

1x

1x

1x

2x

2x

4x

1x

2x

6x

2x

6x

2x

1x

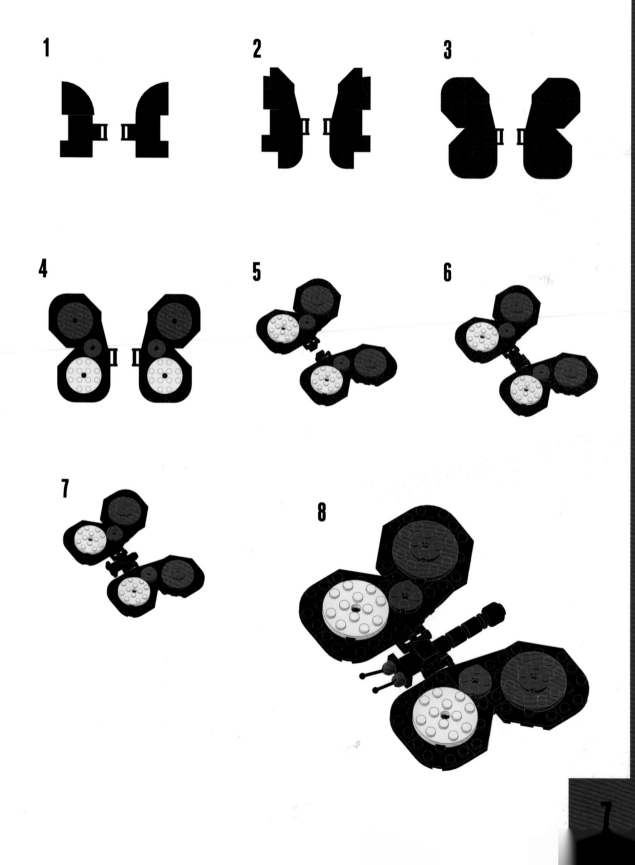

parrot

These brightly coloured birds are found in most tropical and sub-tropical regions and have curved bills, strong legs and clawed feet. Most parrots are vegetarian, living off a diet of seeds, nuts, fruits and other plants. They are among the most intelligent birds on Earth, and domesticated parrots are known for repeating what their owners say. LEGO®'s blue and yellow are the perfect colours for our parrot.

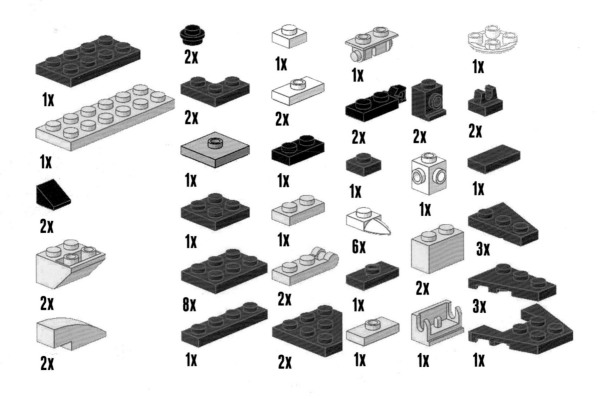

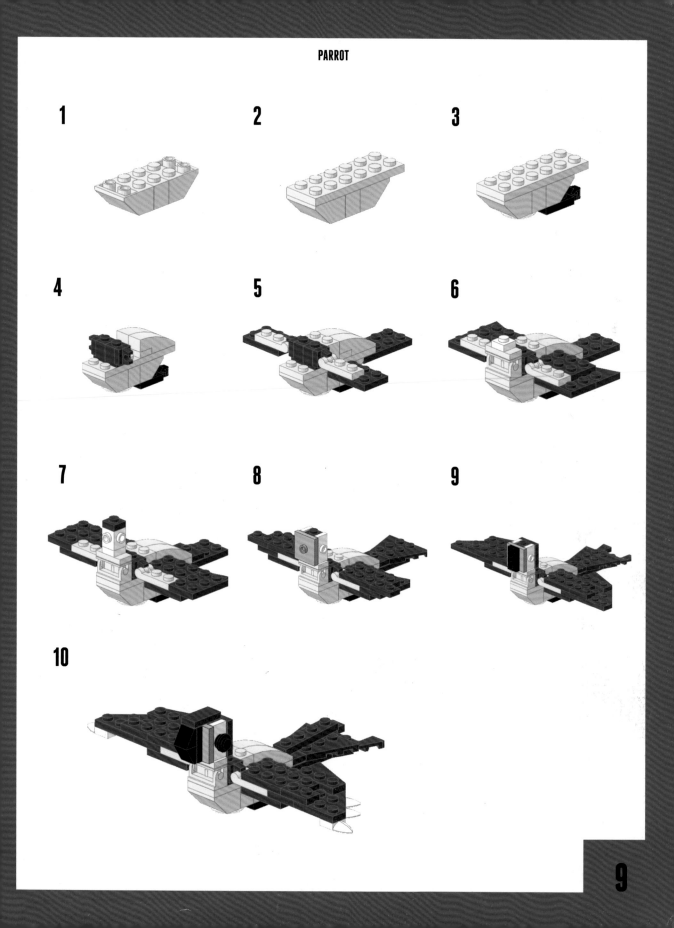

raccoon

Raccoons are most easily identified by their black eye patches and bushy tails — complete with black and white ring markings. In fact, they are often called 'ringtails' because of this. They are nocturnal animals with slender, dexterous front paws. Most commonly found in North America, raccoons are inquisitive and intelligent. Our raccoon's striped tail and legs are depicted with 1 x 1 round plates and 1 x 1 plates.

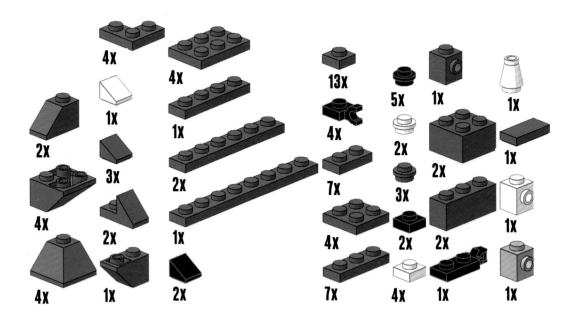

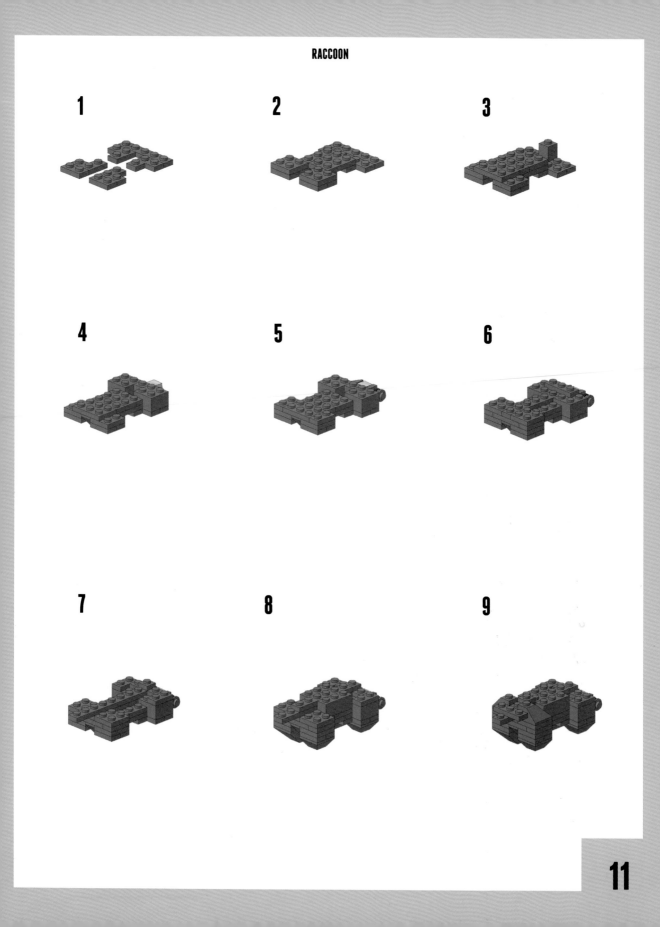

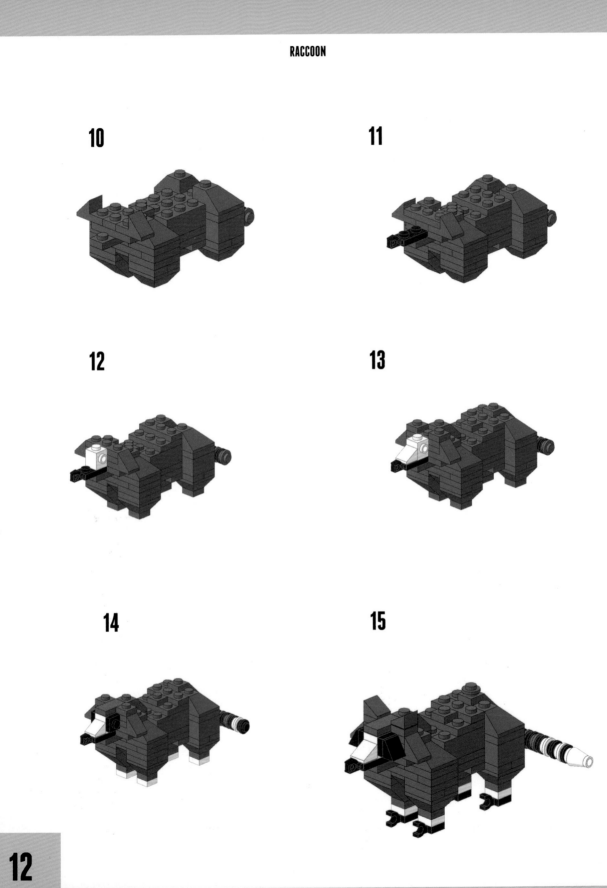

10

11

12

13

14

15

lion

Lions are one of the largest members of the cat family, only beaten by the tiger. Although often referred to as the 'King of the Jungle', they're actually found on the savannas of Africa. Lions are carnivorous mammals that are mainly active at night, spending their days living in small family groups called prides. LEGO® brown and yellow aptly capture the colours of a lion's fur and mane. We've used a variety of regular and inverted 45-degree slopes to give our lion a big mane.

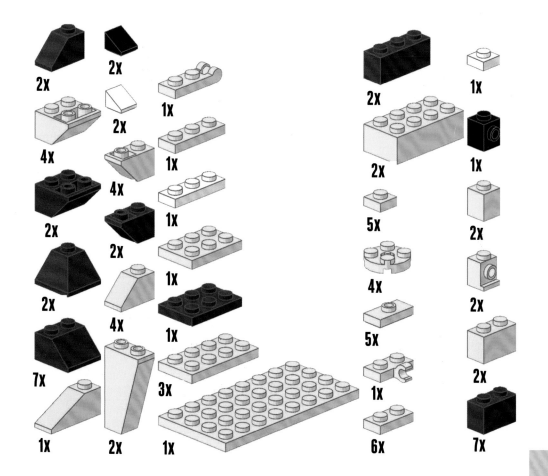

2x

2x

2x

1x

4x

2x

1x

2x

4x

1x

2x

1x

2x

1x

2x

1x

2x

1x

7x

4x

1x

3x

1x

2x

1x

2x

1x

2x

5x

1x

4x

2x

5x

2x

1x

2x

6x

7x

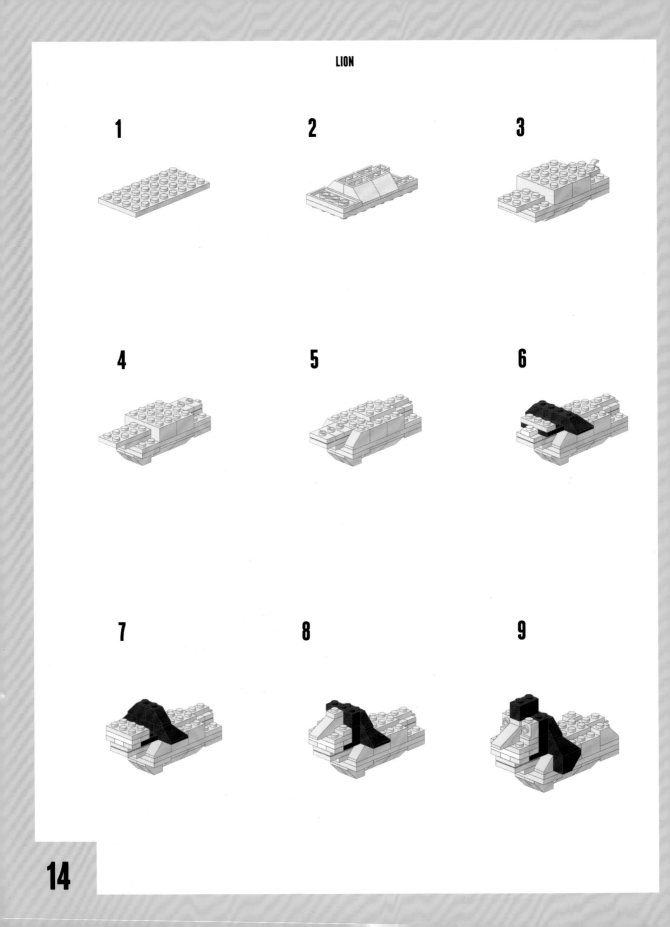

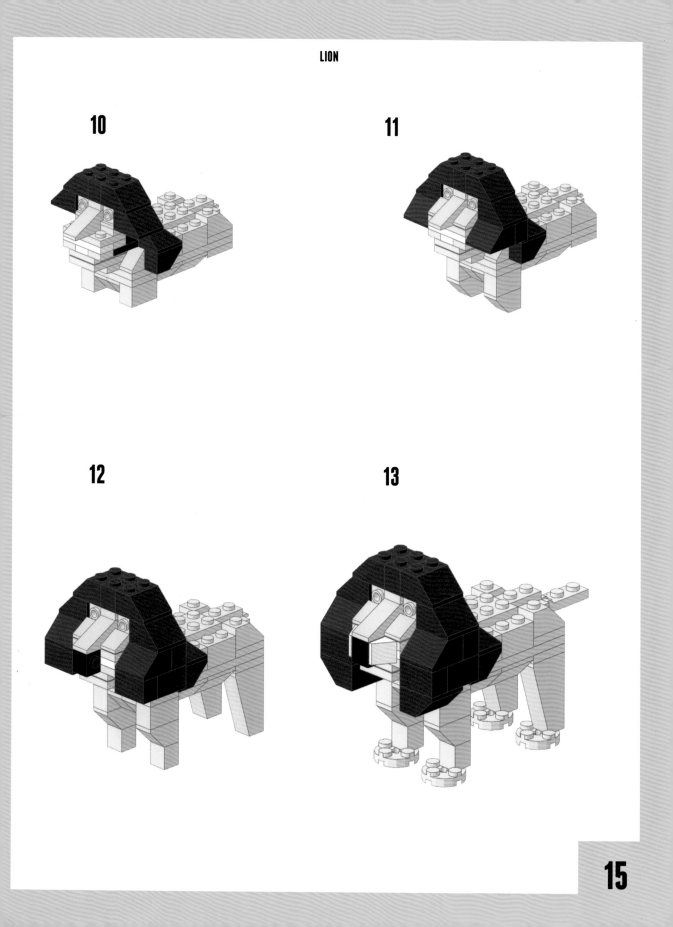

10

11

12

13

rabbit

There are only about 28 species of rabbit in the world, but they live across a surprisingly wide range of habitats, from deserts and tropical forests to wetlands and temperate climates. One of the rabbit's most distinctive features is its long ears, adapted to give it the best chance to hear predators. Rabbits have powerful hind legs, short tails and long claws for digging their underground burrows.

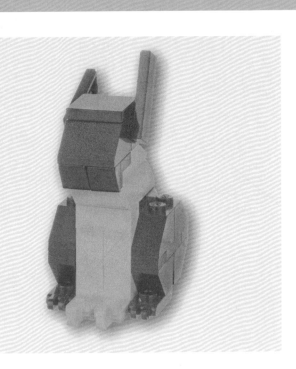

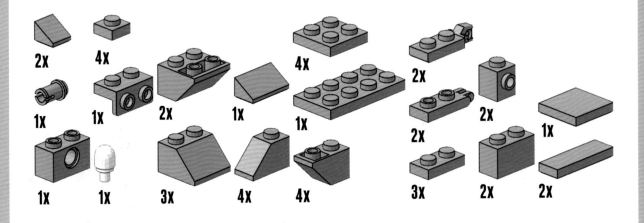

2x 4x 4x 2x

1x 1x 2x 1x 1x 2x 2x 1x

1x 1x 3x 4x 4x 3x 2x 2x

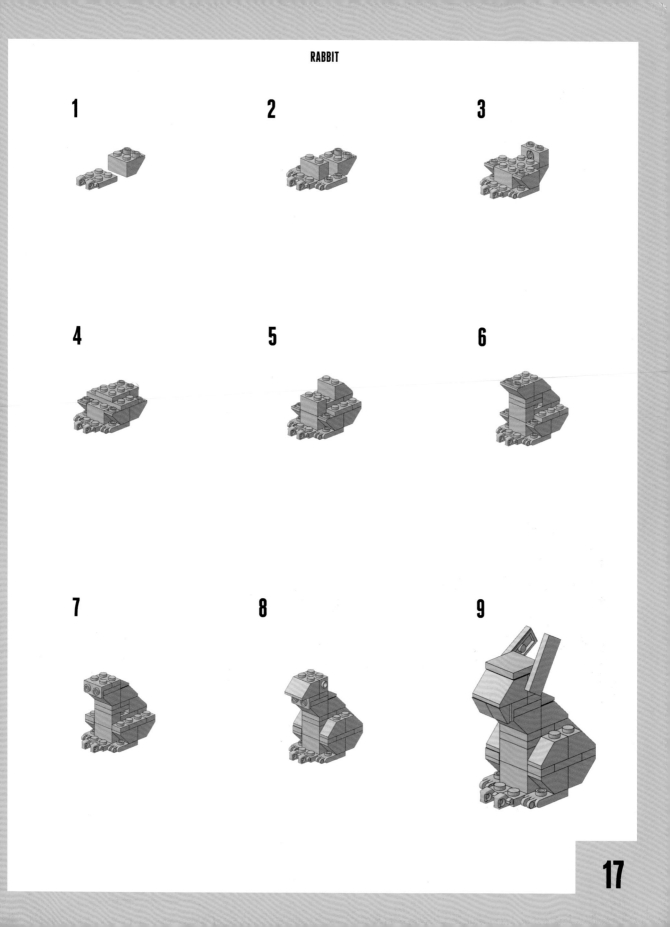

1

2

3

4

5

6

7

8

9

duck

Ducks definitely waddle when they walk! This is because their legs – like swans' – are set far back on their bodies. The mallard, one of the most commonly known species of duck, was first domesticated 2,500 years ago in China. Male ducks differ from their female counterparts in their calls and plumage, with the males getting the colourful, beautiful feathers. We've built a large white duck with yellow legs, feet and bill, known as the Pekin duck.

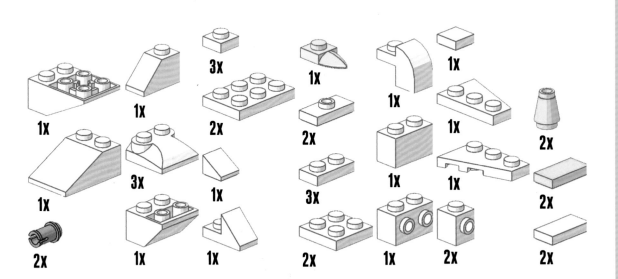

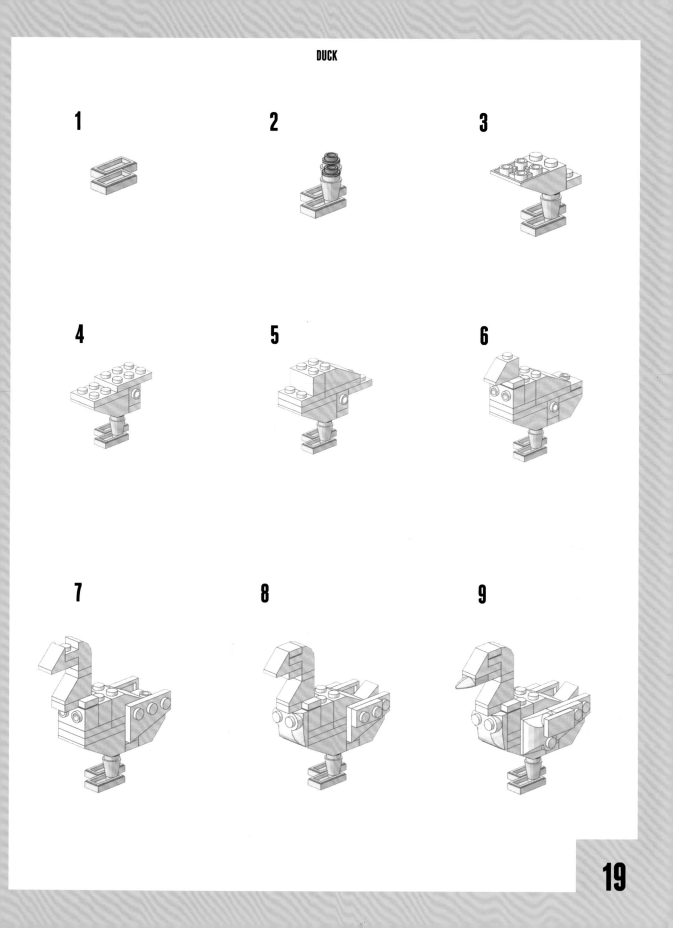

1

2

3

4

5

6

7

8

9

beetle

There are more species of beetle than any other type of insect – 360,000 have been discovered so far, all over the world! They have two pairs of wings; the outer wings are usually hard so as to protect the inner wings. Beetles come in a huge variety of colours, with some sporting sensational patterns. These green tiles are a brilliant way to show the smooth, shiny surfaces of this beetle's body. The six 1 × 4 plates-with-hinge let us create the three pairs of legs.

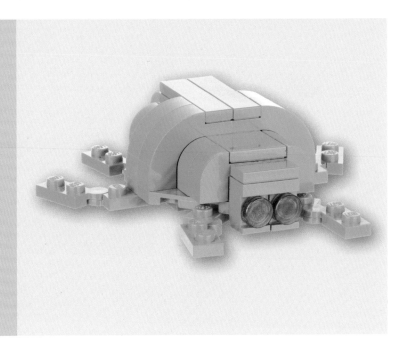

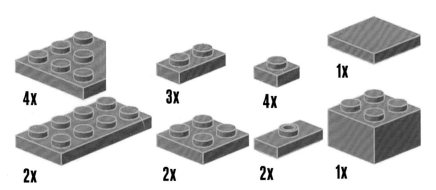

4x   3x   4x   1x

2x   2x   2x   1x

2x   1x   2x   6x

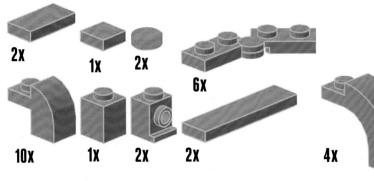

10x   1x   2x   2x   4x

BEETLE

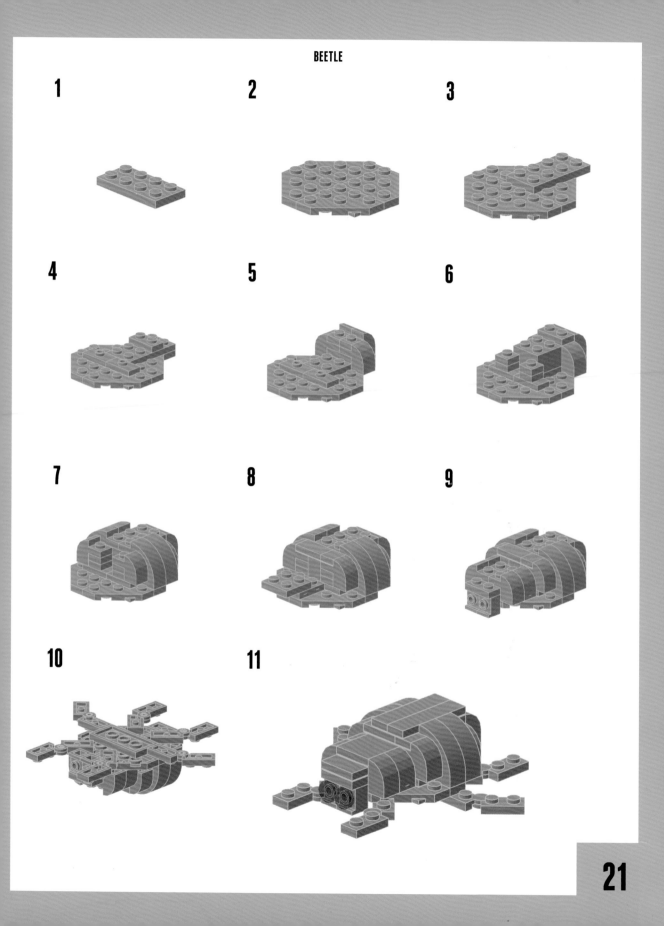

polar bear

Polar bears may seem cute and cuddly, but they are dangerous predators that wouldn't hesitate to kill any humans who cross their path. They live in the Arctic and have the most amazing fur; each hair is a hollow tube that reflects light, making them look very white. Their skin is black, and beneath it is a thick layer of fat, which helps keep them warm in their freezing habitat. We've used 2 × 2, 72-degree slopes to imitate the shoulders and haunches of our polar bear.

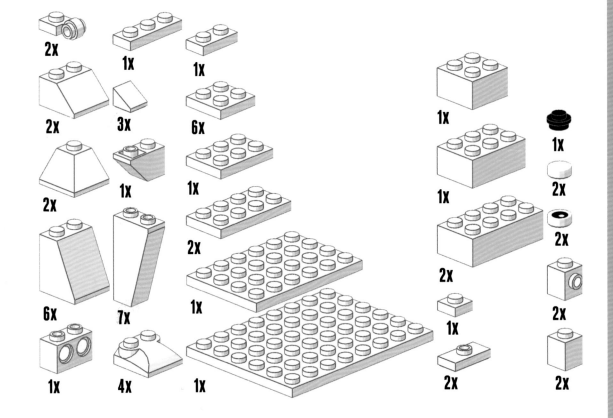

2x 1x 1x

2x 3x 6x 1x

2x 1x 1x 1x 2x

6x 7x 1x 2x 2x

1x 4x 1x 2x 2x

POLAR BEAR

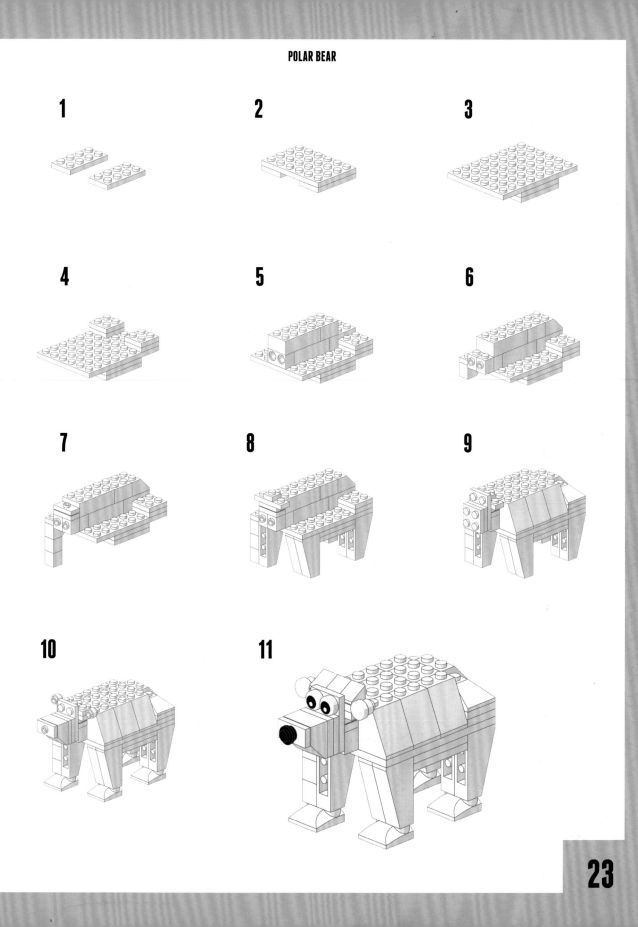

fox

Foxes are part of the dog family, but are differentiated by their pointed ears, narrow noses and bushy tails. Red foxes are found in more parts of the world than any other animal, except humans. Originally only found in the countryside, foxes are now common in some cities, where they survive by scavenging scraps of rubbish and food. They are around 1m (3 ft) long when fully grown, with just under half of that length being their tail!

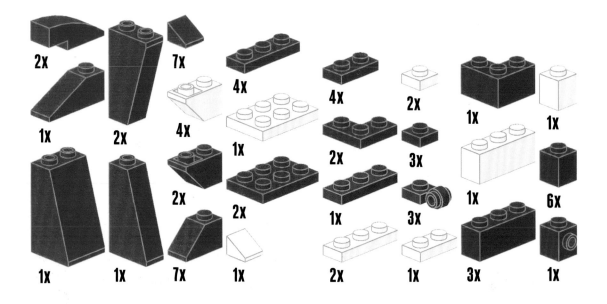

2x

1x 2x 7x

1x 1x 7x

4x

4x

1x

2x

2x

4x

2x

1x

2x

1x

3x

3x

2x

2x

1x

1x

3x

1x

1x

1x

6x

3x

1x

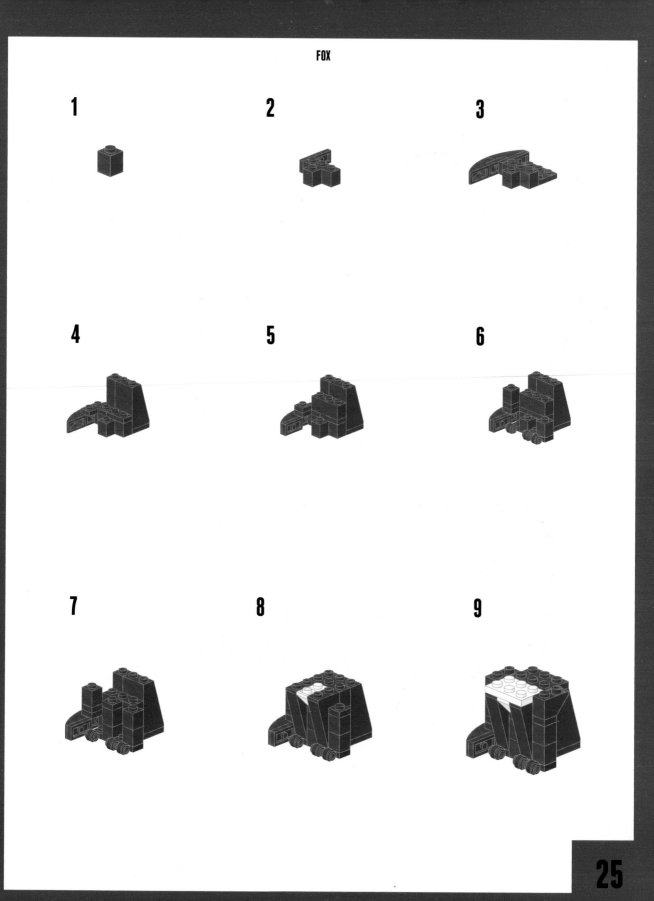

10

11

12

13

14

15

elephant

Elephants are the world's largest living land mammals. With their long trunks, tusks and big ears, you certainly wouldn't miss one coming your way! They live in family groups, headed by the lead female, and can live until they're about 60 years old. Elephants spend up to 18 hours a day eating, and only sleep in short bursts. LEGO® dark grey is perfect for our elephant, and we have lots of useful parts in this colour with which to build it.

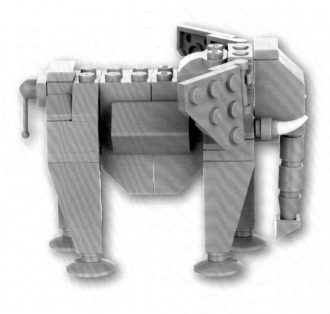

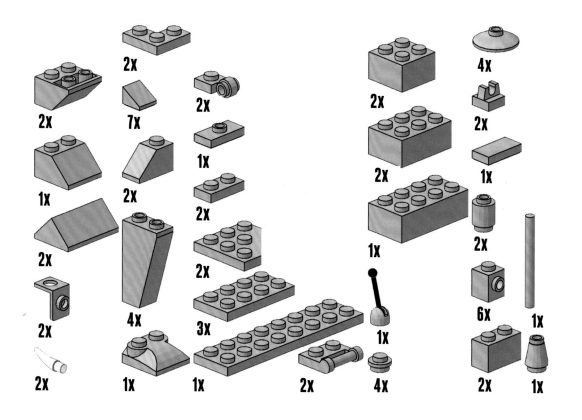

2x · 2x · 7x · 2x · 1x · 2x · 2x · 1x · 2x · 2x · 4x · 4x · 2x · 2x · 1x · 2x · 2x · 3x · 2x · 1x · 4x · 6x · 1x · 2x · 1x

1

2

3

4

5

6

7

8

9

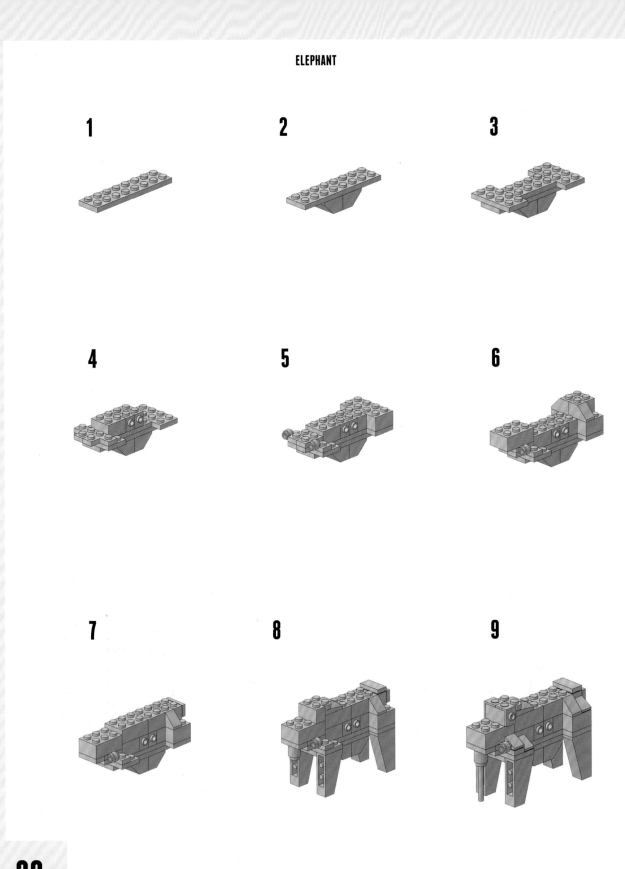

10

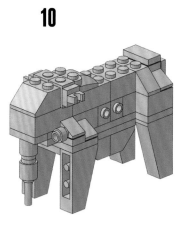

11

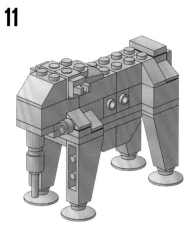

12

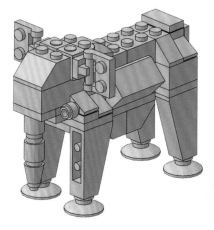

13

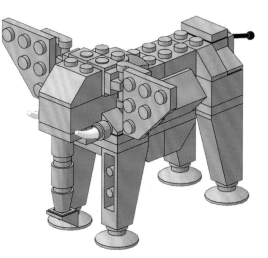

panda

Giant pandas are large bears with distinctive black and white markings. Males can reach 1.8 m (6 ft) in length and weigh more than 100 kg (220 lb). When they're not eating bamboo, they love tumbling, dust bathing and somersaulting in the snow. Although they look a bit clumsy, they are good at climbing trees. Their markings and cute appearance have endeared them to the world, but they are one of the most endangered species on the planet.

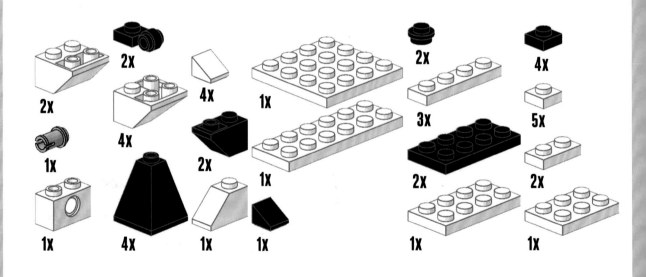

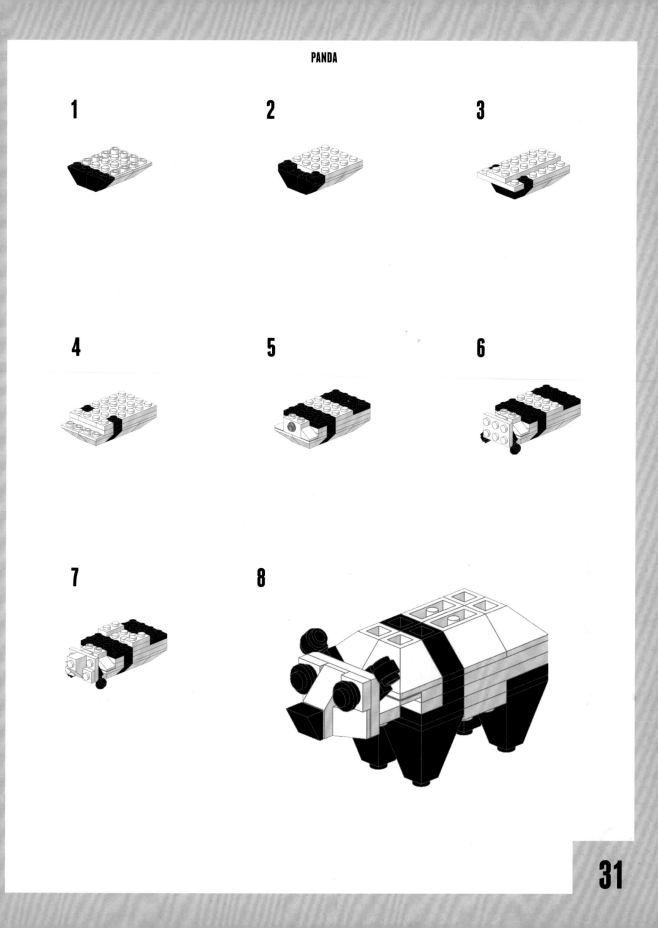

seal

There are about 30 species of seal, living mostly in cold seas. They are mammals, with webbed feet, flippers and tapered bodies, so while they're slow on land, they're the perfect shape for swimming! A thick layer of blubber protects them from the cold. Seals are carnivores, living on fish, squid, molluscs and crustaceans. This one's hind flippers are built using 1 x 4 plate-hinges; its forward flippers are mirror-imaged 2 x 6 curved wedge bricks.

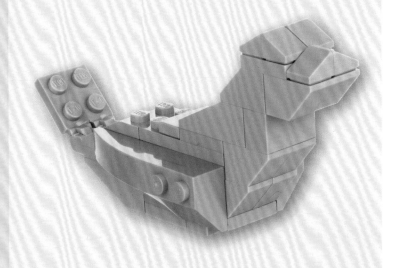

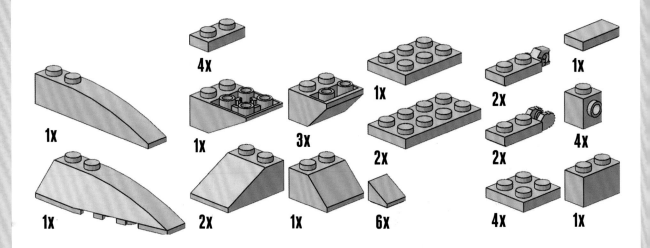

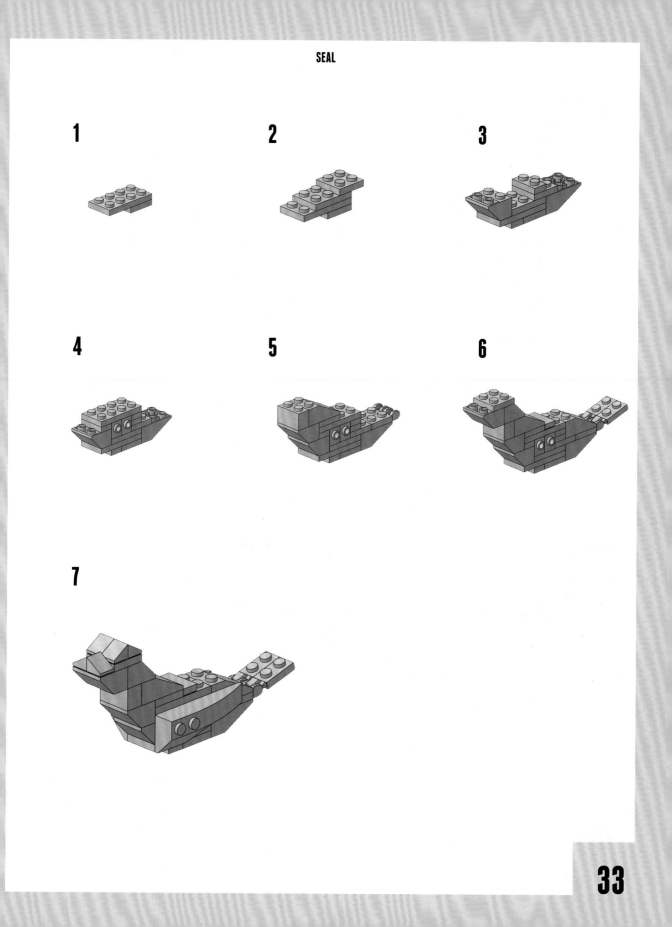

1

2

3

4

5

6

7

bumblebee

The transparent pieces were the inspiration for this bee. The smoky black colour immediately jumped out as the piece to make wings from. Of course, a real bee would have very thin wings, but our LEGO® bee is a cute fellow, and he promises not to sting you. I needed to reverse the direction the studs were pointing to make his tail, which is achieved by putting a lightsaber blade inside two round bricks.

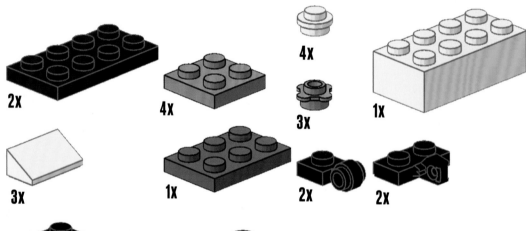

2x

4x

4x

3x

1x

3x

1x

2x

2x

1x

3x

4x

2x

4x

4x

3x

2x

4x

1x

1x

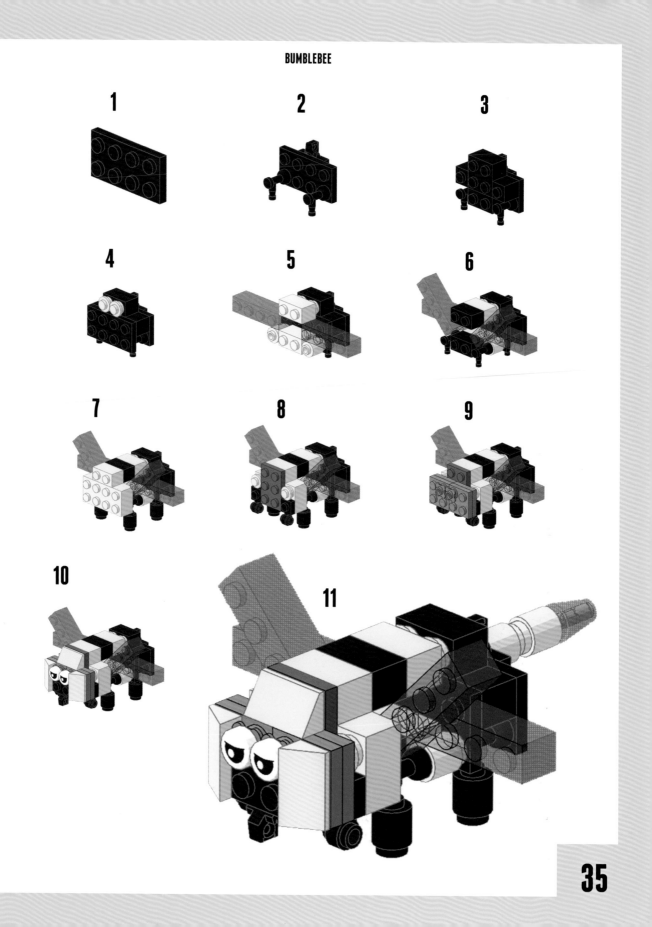

piranha

Piranhas live in rivers and lakes in South America, and although they have very sharp and strong teeth, they are, thankfully, not quite as vicious as their reputation would have you believe! Piranhas have large, blunt heads, and their teeth are triangular and work like scissors. For our model, we've built one of the most common colourings of the species, with a silvery-grey upper half and orange belly. We've used a 2 x 2, 65-degree slope to give the distinctive head shape.

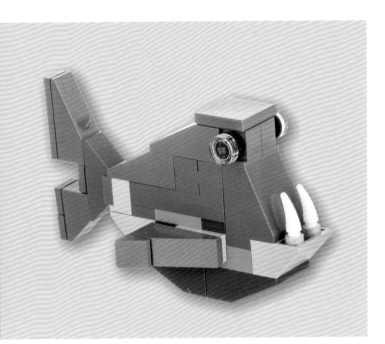

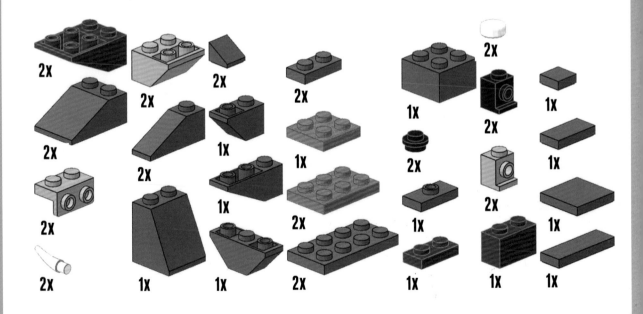

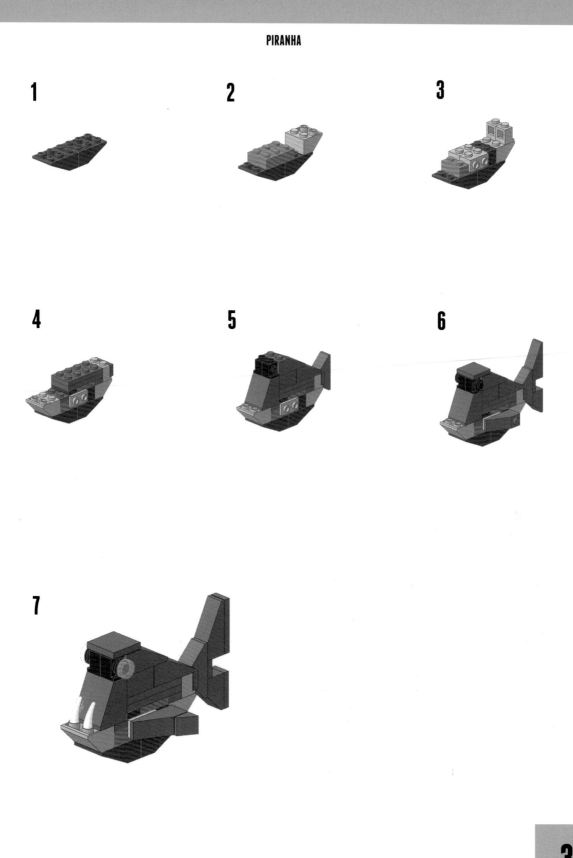

goat

As brought to life by the Norwegian fairy tale 'Three Billy Goats Gruff', male goats have a beard and hooves to rap-tap-tap along the ground. Goats are closely related to sheep, but are less heavily built, have shorter tails, and horns that arch backwards. They are domesticated in many parts of the world, mainly because of their milk, which is also made into cheese. We've used two 1 x 1 plates-with-clip to represent the goat's horns, and a small slope recreates the beard.

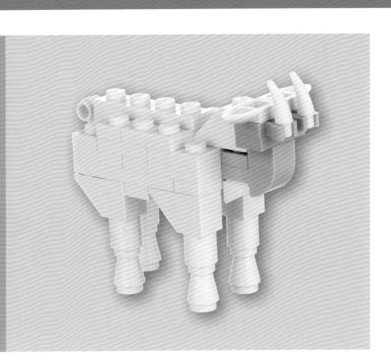

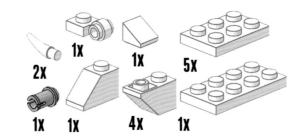

2x 1x 1x 5x

1x 1x 4x 1x

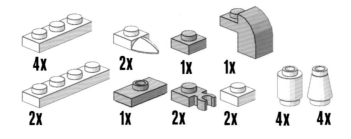

4x 2x 1x 1x

2x 1x 2x 2x 4x 4x

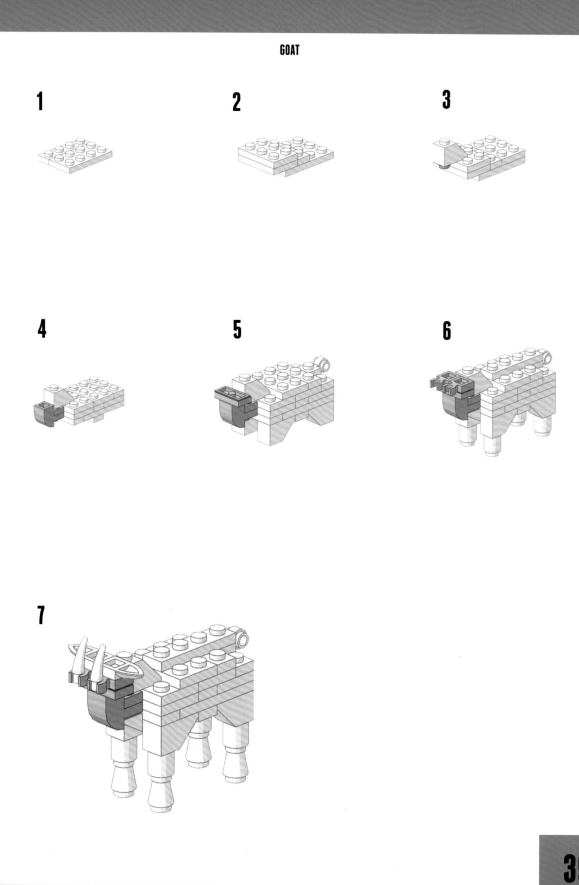

snake

Lots of people are afraid of snakes; this fear is known as ophidiophobia. These reptiles slither from place to place, and their lack of eyelids makes them look like they're staring. They have a long, thin tongue that makes a hissing sound as it darts in and out. There are about 3,000 species of snakes, and although they are predators, only about one in ten are venomous. We've used 1 x 4 plate-hinges for our snake's body, so it can sit up to show off its curves.

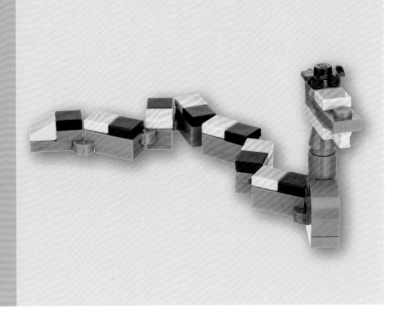

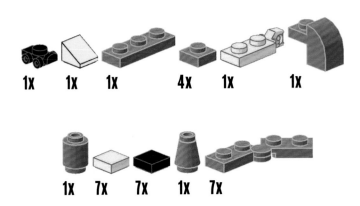

1x   1x   1x   4x   1x   1x

1x   7x   7x   1x   7x

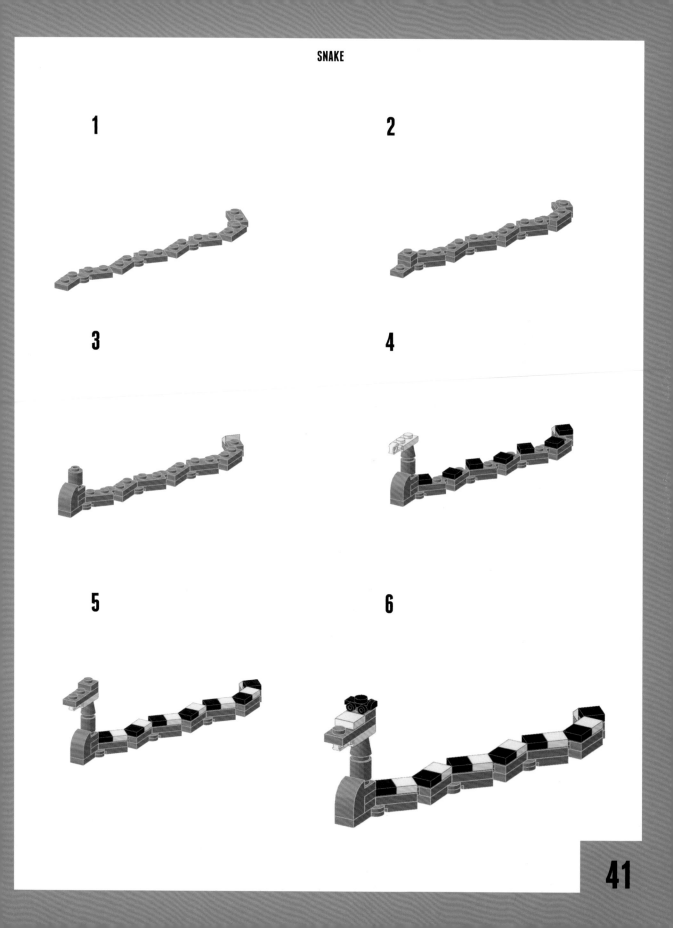

cat

The cat is one of our favourite house pets, with more than 70 domesticated breeds. They have strong, flexible bodies and sharp claws and teeth, all adapted to help them catch small prey. They are carnivorous animals and love to hunt for birds or mice. Their excellent hearing, night vision and highly developed sense of smell mean they make good predators too. However, they're just as comfortable at home with a warm lap to sleep on.

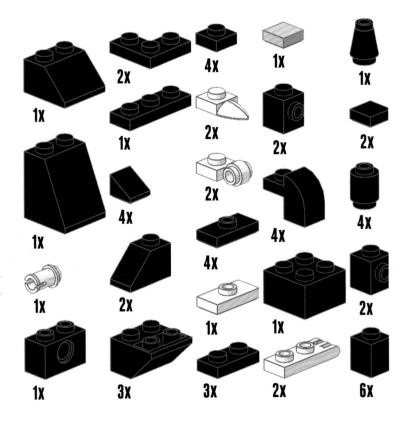

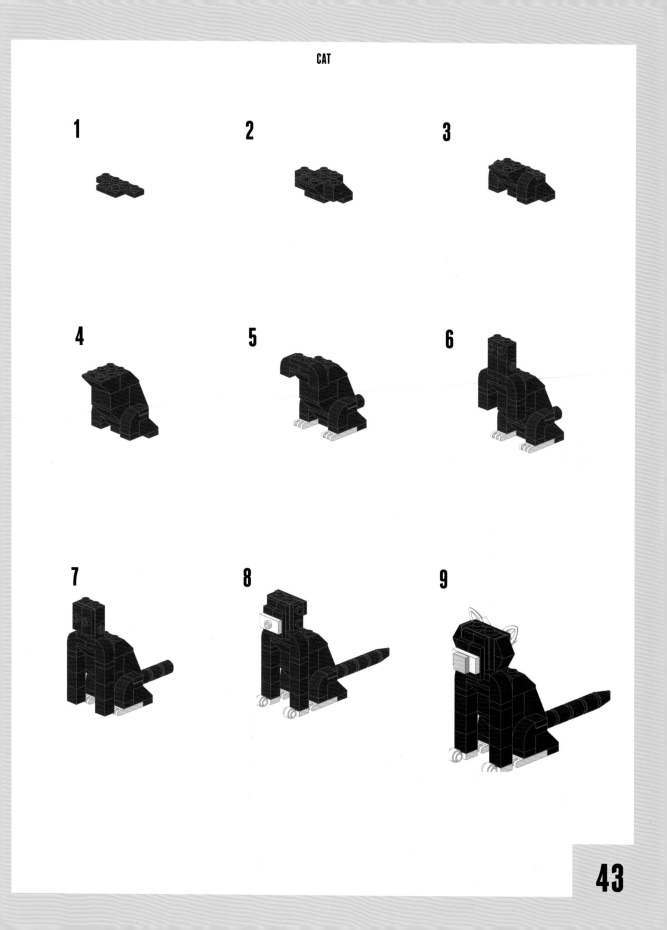

1

2

3

4

5

6

7

8

9

pig

Pigs are omnivores and will happily eat almost anything. Many are domesticated and farmed for their meat, but pigs and boars also live in the wild. They are usually pink with a curly tail, floppy ears, and a long snout for searching out food. As well as eating, pigs love to roll around in the mud. The 2 × 2 double-convex 65-degree slope used here is perfect for the classic shape of a pig's snout, and is finished off with a 1 × 1 round plate for its button nose.

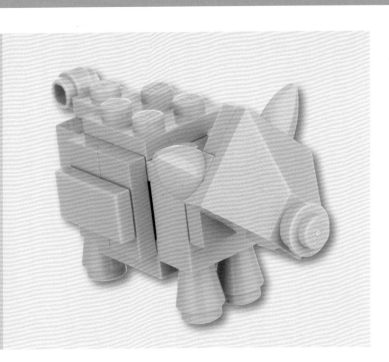

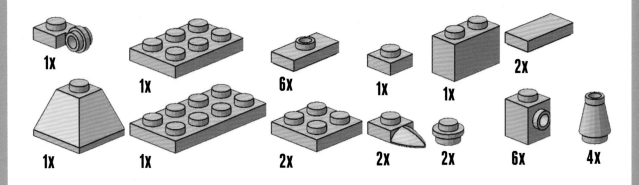

1x   1x   6x   1x   1x   2x

1x   1x   2x   2x   2x   6x   4x

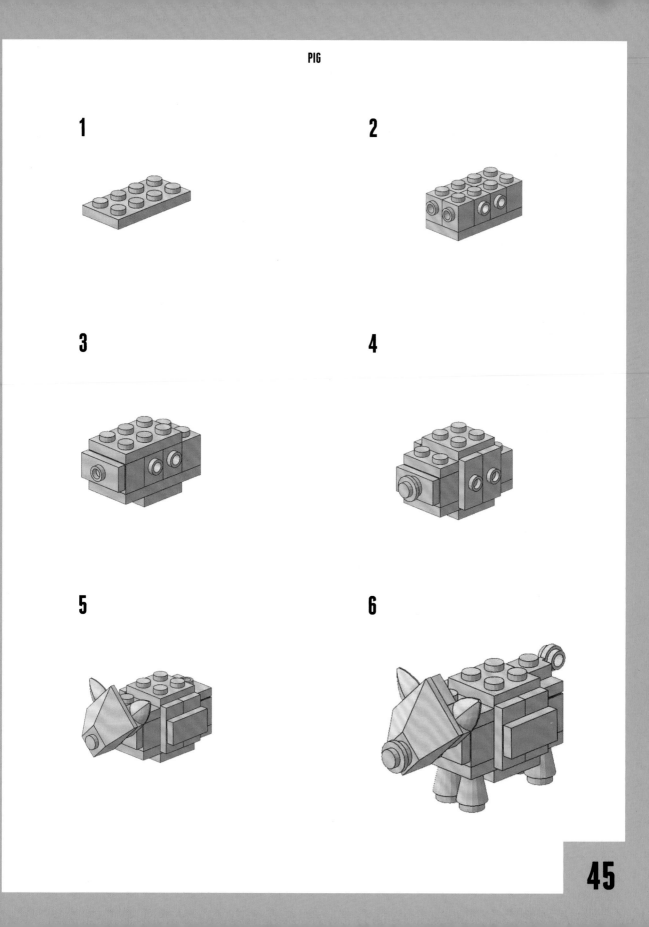

1

2

3

4

5

6

sheep

Sheep are cud-chewing mammals. Many species have been domesticated and are farmed for their wool, which is sheared off each year. They are also bred for meat, and as with cows, there are many breeds with distinct colourings, such as the Merino, originally from Spain, known for its particularly fine and soft wool. We've used pale grey Technic half-pins for our sheep's legs to differentiate them from its wool-covered body, and 1 x 1 round tiles for its flat feet.

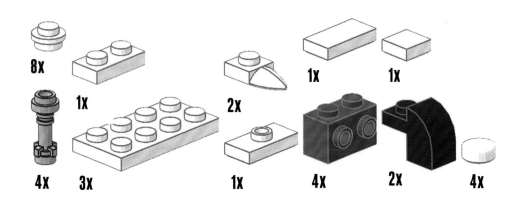

8x

1x

4x   3x

2x

1x

1x   1x

4x   2x   4x

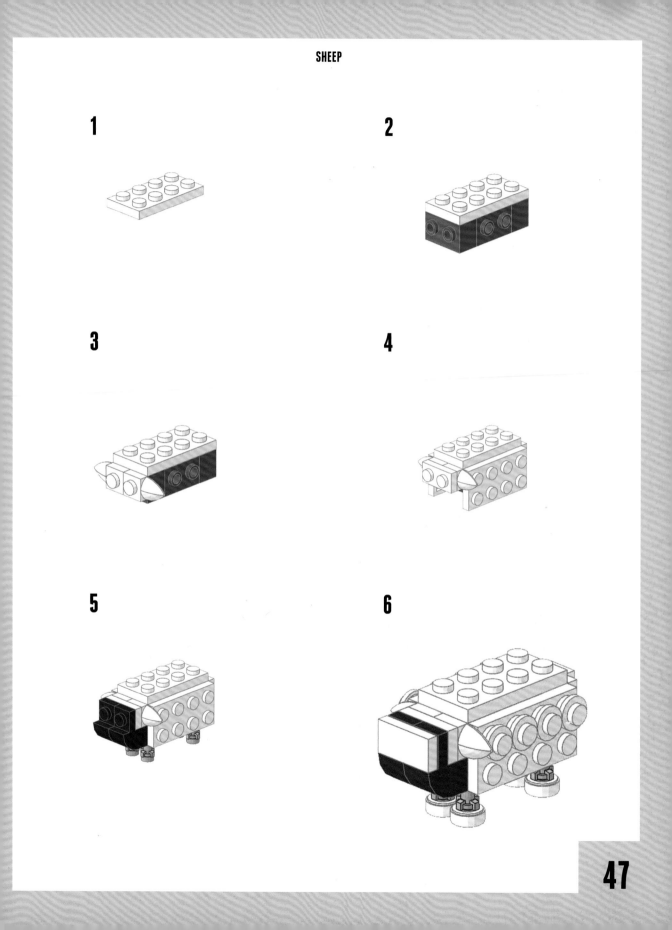

1

2

3

4

5

6

COW

In much of the world, cows are farm animals, bred for their milk, meat or ability to produce calves. However, in India they are revered as a symbol of life and may never be killed. There are lots of breeds of cattle, but we've created our cow from black and white brick and plate pieces. Its snout uses a 1 x 2, 45-degree slope, which is attached sideways, topped off by a pink 1 x 1 tile. The horns are held in place by 1 x 1 plates with lamp holders.

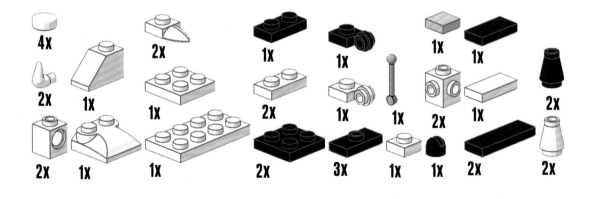

4x

2x

1x

1x

1x

1x

2x

1x

1x

2x

1x

1x

2x

2x

1x

1x

1x

2x

1x

3x

1x

1x

2x

2x

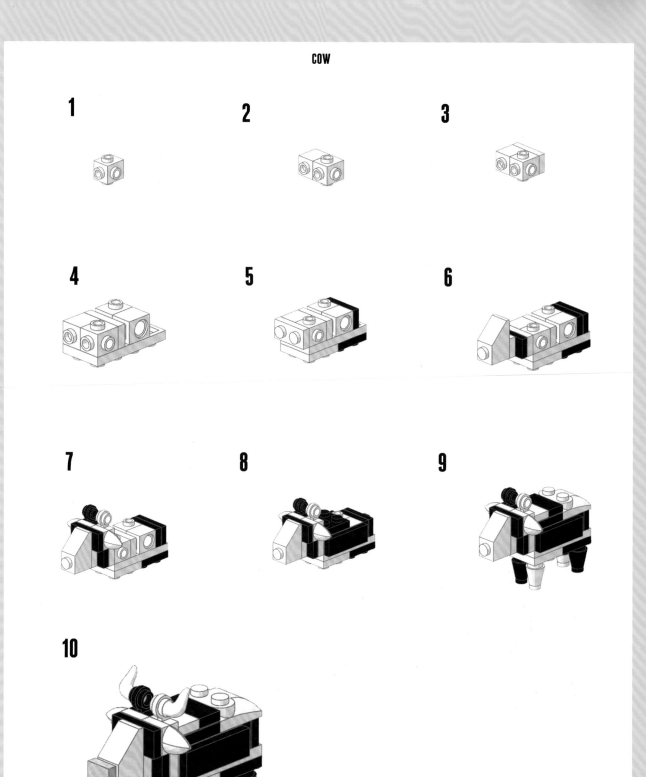

stork

Storks are large wading birds with long legs and necks. They have huge bills, but no voice-box, so they don't make any vocal sounds. Instead, they make a clattering noise with their beak. Many species are migratory and use a soaring, gliding method of flight to travel long distances. A combination of 2 × 2, 45-degree slopes in white and 1 × 3, 33-degree slopes in black recreate our stork's wings and the change in plumage colour.

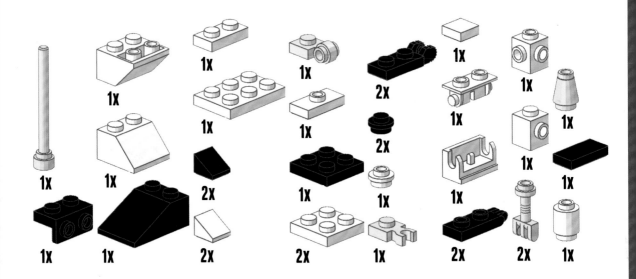

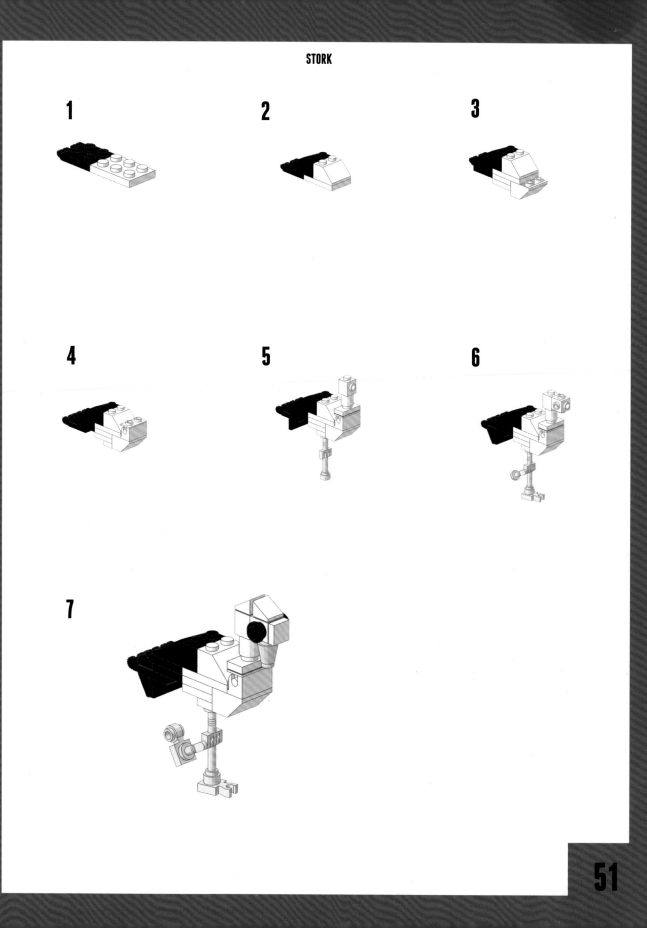

lobster

Lobsters are crustaceans. They are mostly nocturnal, scavenging food and eating small, live fish and seaweed. They have five pairs of legs and large claws. Females breed at about five years old, laying up to 3,000 eggs at a time. Here we've used long radio aerials for the prominent antennae, and taps for the non-clawed legs. Special slopes, designed for roof ridge ends, are perfect for the sectioned back shell.

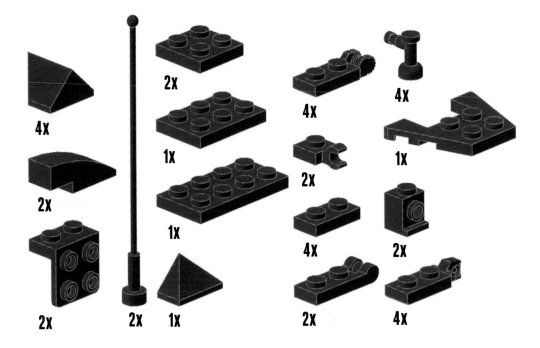

4x

2x

2x

2x 2x 1x

2x

1x

1x

4x

2x

4x

1x

2x

4x

2x

1x

2x

4x

1

2

3

4

5

6

7

8

9

10

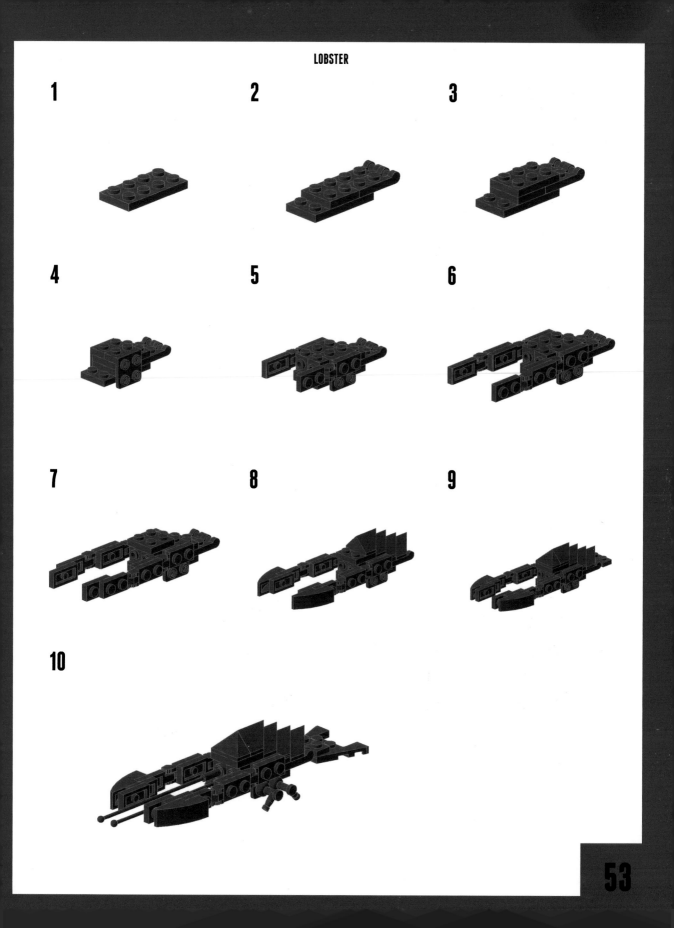

frog

Frogs are amphibians, meaning they live both on land and in water, with long back legs designed for hopping around. They are born in water, developing from eggs – known as frogspawn – to become a tadpole, and finally a frog. Most frogs eat insects or worms, but some eat other frogs, rodents and reptiles. Our frog is LEGO® green with highlights of dark green, and a selection of slopes at different angles allow us to recreate its hind legs.

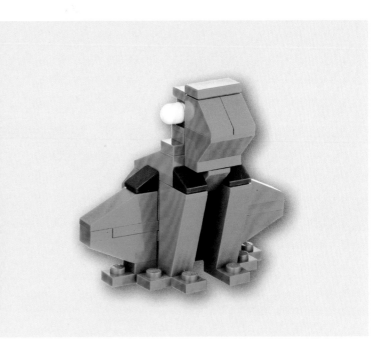

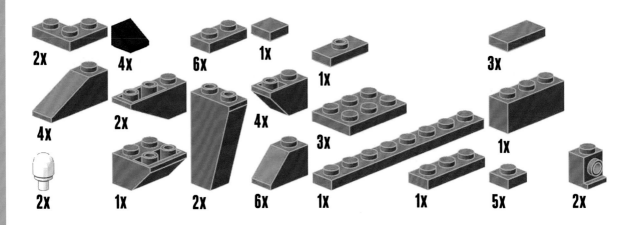

2x 4x 6x 1x 1x 3x

4x 2x 4x 3x 1x

2x 1x 2x 6x 1x 1x 5x 2x

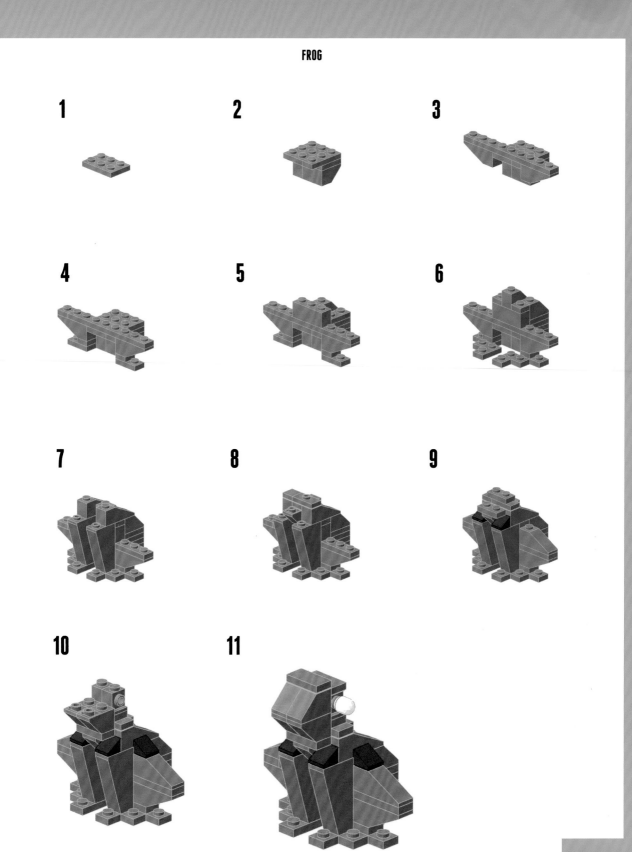

turkey

Turkeys are native to the Americas. Male turkeys are heavier than females and have a distinctive fleshy wattle that hangs from the top of their beak. Turkey is the traditional main dish for Christmas in the United Kingdom. We've given our turkey its archetypal blue and red colourings for its head and wattle. Its characteristic tail has been crafted using a stack of 2 × 2 and 3 × 3 inverted dishes, attached at its rear.

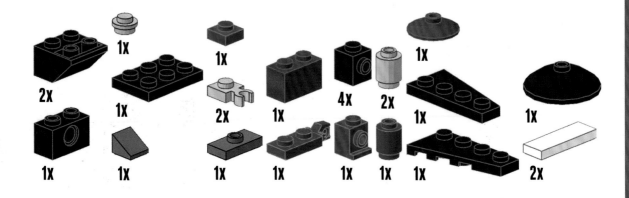

2x   1x   1x   1x   2x   1x   4x   2x   1x   1x

1x   1x   1x   1x   1x   1x   1x   2x

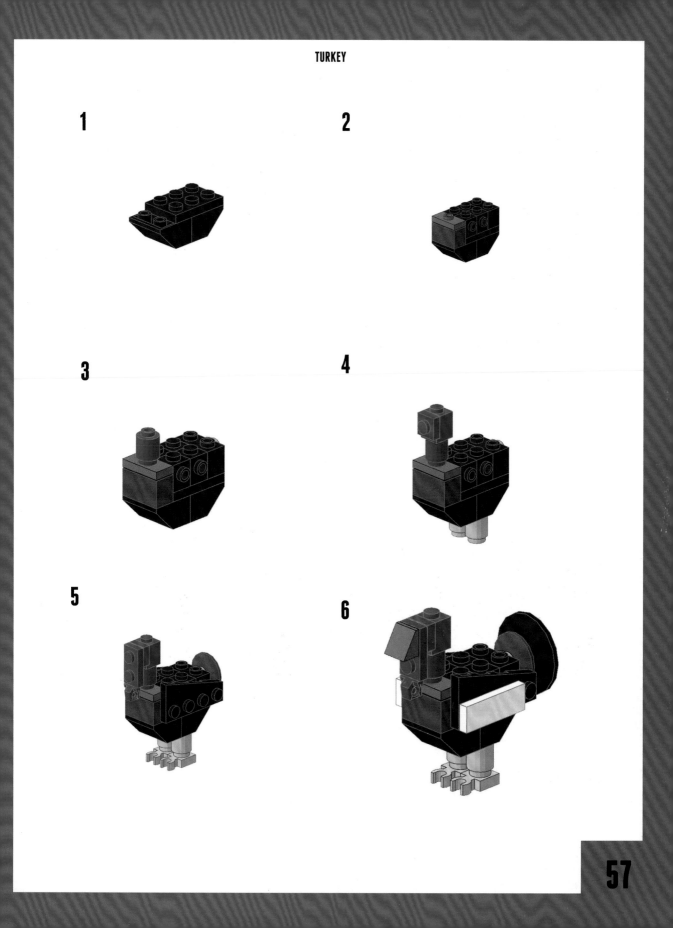

shark

Sharks are one of the world's most feared animals. Steven Spielberg's movie *Jaws* depicted them as dangerous, and while they have been known to attack humans, most species are harmless. Sharks are recognizable by the gills on the sides of their heads and a triangular dorsal fin rising above the waves. For our model, the 3 × 3, 45-degree wedge plate is the ideal piece for our shark's iconic fin. Its tail is made from a 2 × 2 × 2 cone and a selection of different slopes.

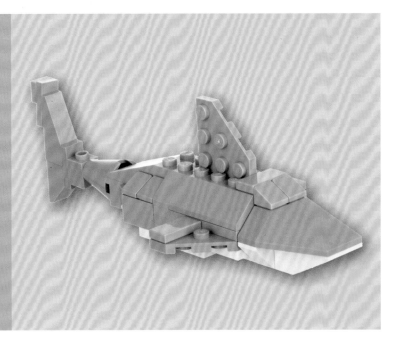

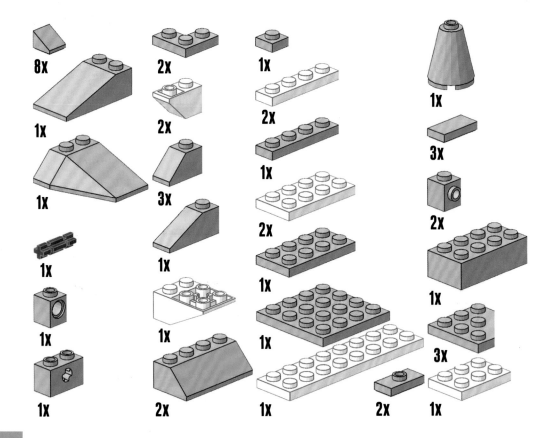

8x

1x

1x

1x

1x

2x

2x

3x

1x

1x

2x

2x

1x

2x

1x

1x

1x

1x

2x

1x

3x

2x

1x

1x

2x

1x

3x

1x

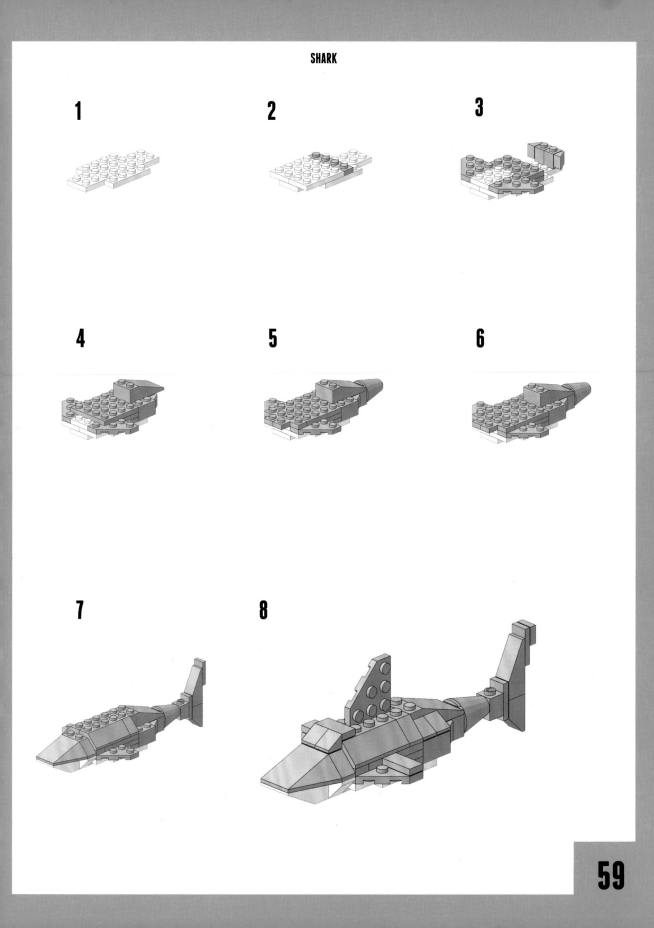

horse

Horses have been used by humans for centuries for all kinds of purposes. Before the mechanization of vehicles, horses were used in farming and transportation. This is where the term 'horse power' comes from to describe the power of a vehicle. Today, horses are ridden for leisure, tourism and sport. We've used a variety of slopes for the shoulders, haunches and neck, and 1 x 1 plates-with-tooth for the ears and feet.

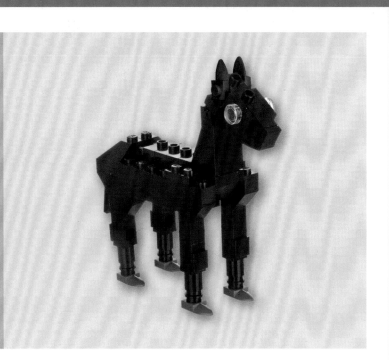

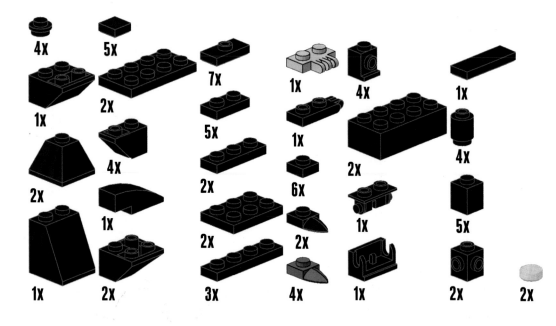

4x 5x 7x 1x 4x 1x

1x 2x 5x 1x 4x

2x 4x 2x 6x 2x 4x

1x 1x 2x 2x 1x 5x

1x 2x 3x 4x 1x 2x 2x

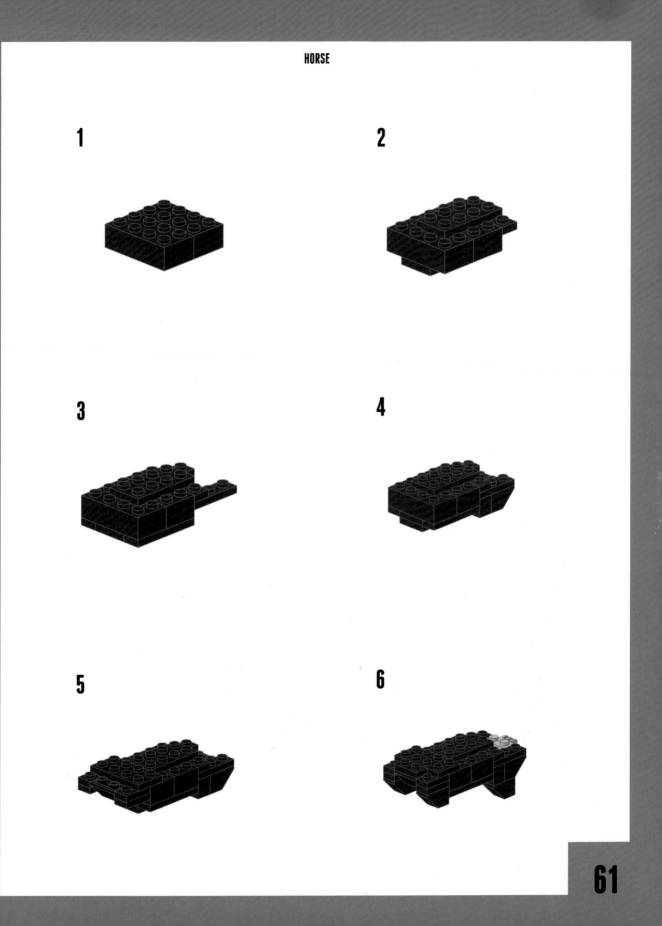

giraffe

Giraffes are the tallest living mammals, often growing over 5.5 m (19 ft) tall. Despite their size, they are able to run very fast when they need to. They have also evolved long necks to be able to reach their food. Here we've used LEGO® minifigure heads for the knobby knees. When you're building this one, don't worry too much about using brown or yellow pieces – each giraffe is unique, so the pattern can be too!

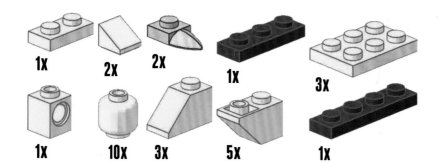

1x 2x 2x 1x 3x

1x 10x 3x 5x 1x

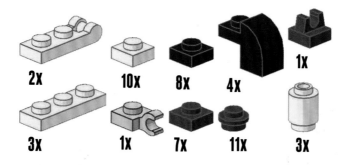

2x 10x 8x 4x 1x

3x 1x 7x 11x 3x

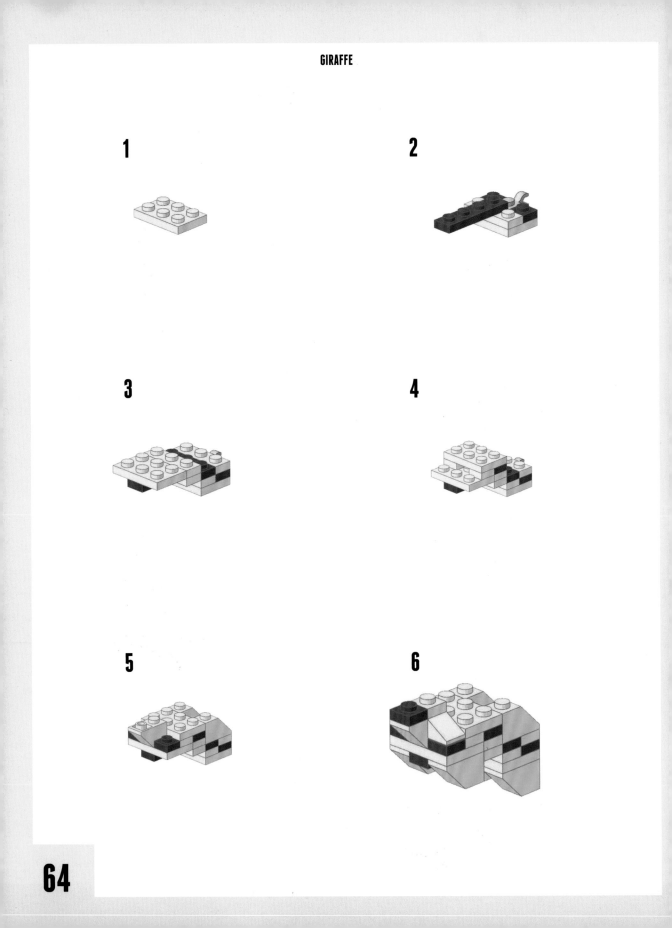

1

2

3

4

5

6

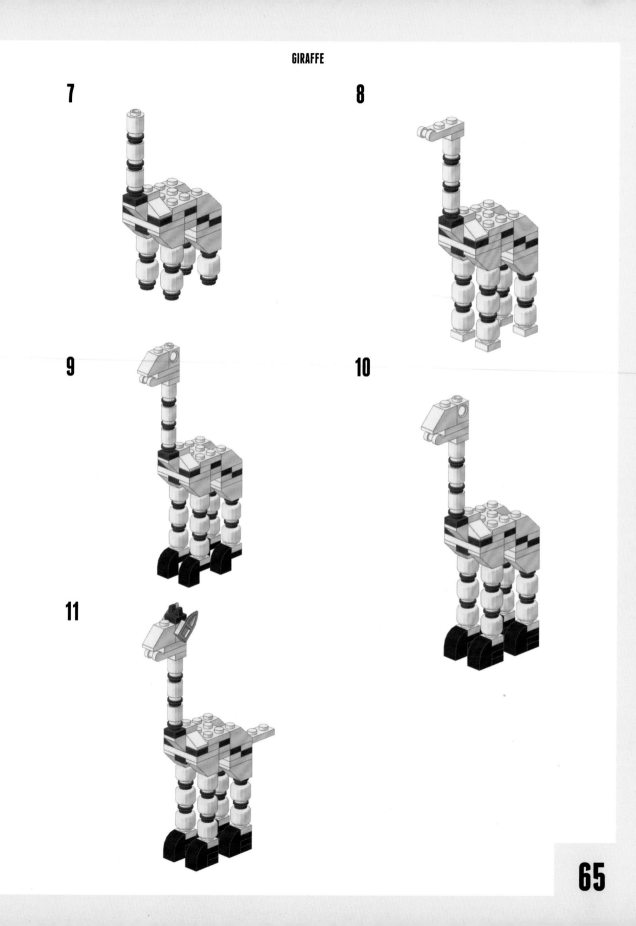

7

8

9

10

11

camel

The camel's most distinctive feature is its hump – some have one hump and others have two. Contrary to popular belief, the humps are not full of water; they are made up of fat, allowing the desert beast to trek for days without food. The curvy shape of our one-humped camel – known as a dromedary – has been recreated using both regular and inverted 45-degree slopes.

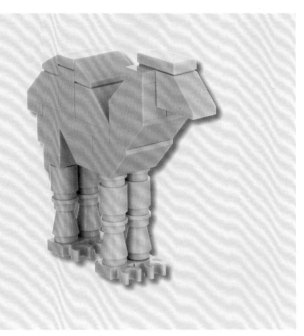

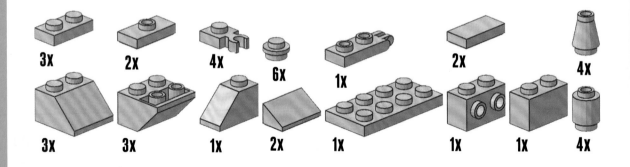

3x 2x 4x 6x 1x 2x 4x

3x 3x 1x 2x 1x 1x 1x 4x

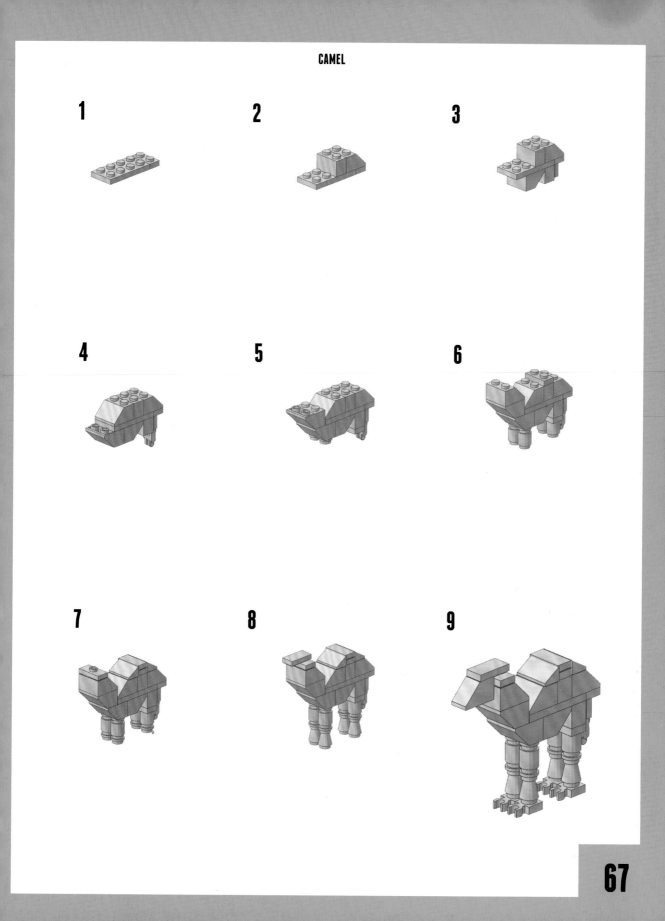

1 **2** **3**

4 **5** **6**

7 **8** **9**

swan

Known as graceful swimmers that glide on the water while being equally capable of breaking your arm, swans are among the largest species of waterfowl. Swans mate for life and will rear their young together. Baby swans are called cygnets; they have mottled brown or grey feathers for the first two years of their lives. We've used a 1 × 2 plate-with-tooth, coupled with a black tile and a 1 × 2 curved brick, to show the distinctive head and bill.

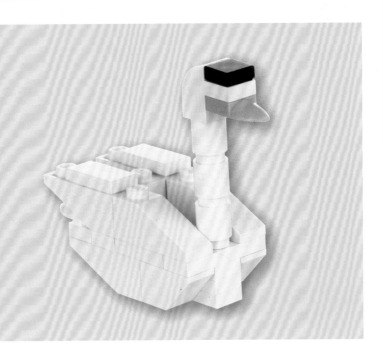

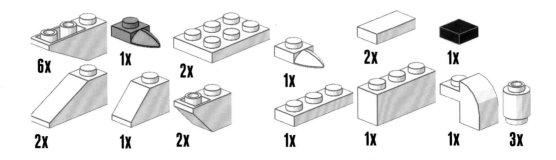

6x   1x   2x   1x   2x   1x

2x   1x   2x   1x   1x   1x   3x

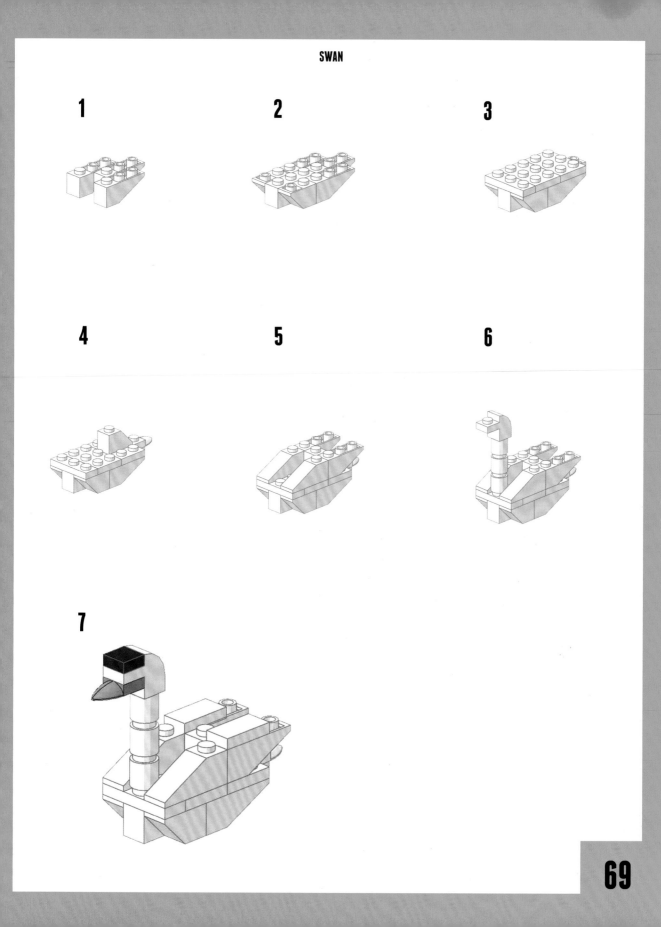

crab

Crabs are crustaceans, which live in hard shells to protect their soft bodies. Usually found on the coast, crabs are mostly omnivores and live by scavenging food. Their front legs have pincers, which they use to eat, for defence and for catching prey. Crabs prefer to move from side to side, scuttling across the beach. We've used levers and lever bases to build the eyes, which sit on stalks – so they can see what's coming from all directions!

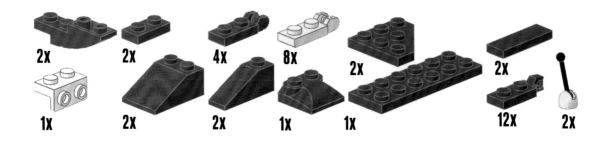

2x **2x** **4x** **8x** **2x** **2x**

1x **2x** **2x** **1x** **1x** **12x** **2x**

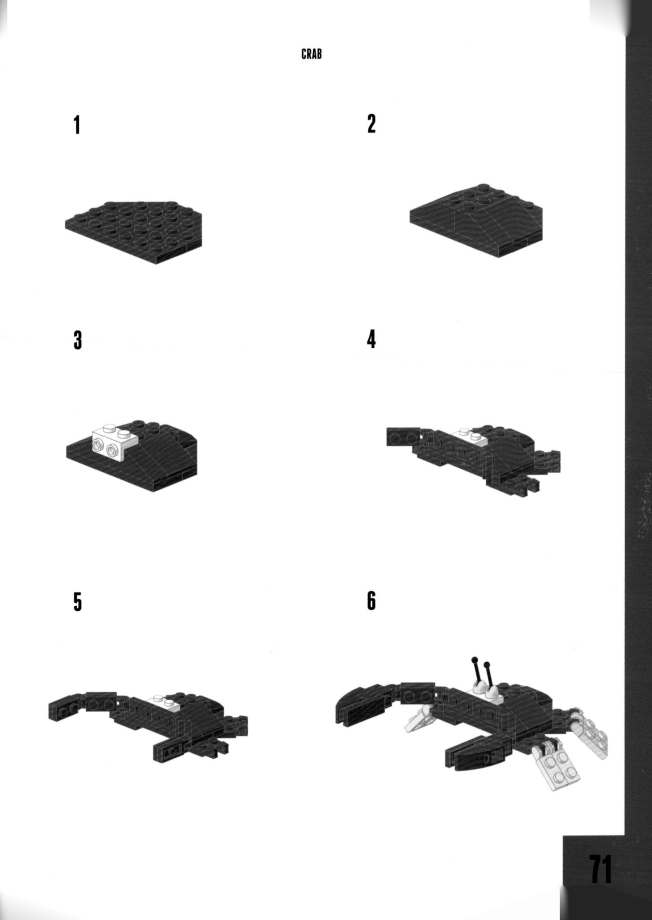

1

2

3

4

5

6

beaver

Beavers are the second largest rodent in the world, native to North America, Europe and Asia. They're hardworking and use their fur-lined lips to work with wood – even underwater! Their lips close behind their chisel-shaped teeth, which are designed to chop wood for their homes. We've used some older pieces – 1 x 4 finger hinges – to show the delicate fingers on the beaver's paws. The different coloured tiles distinguish the tail and fur.

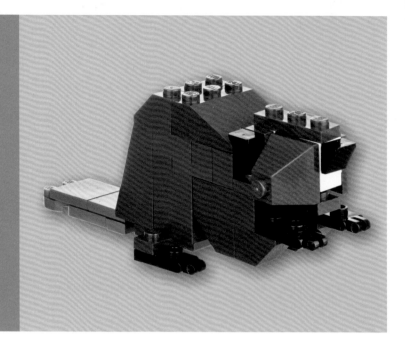

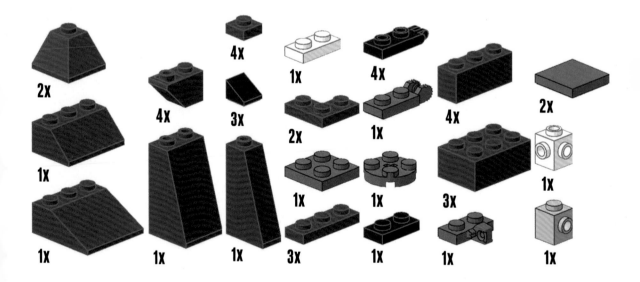

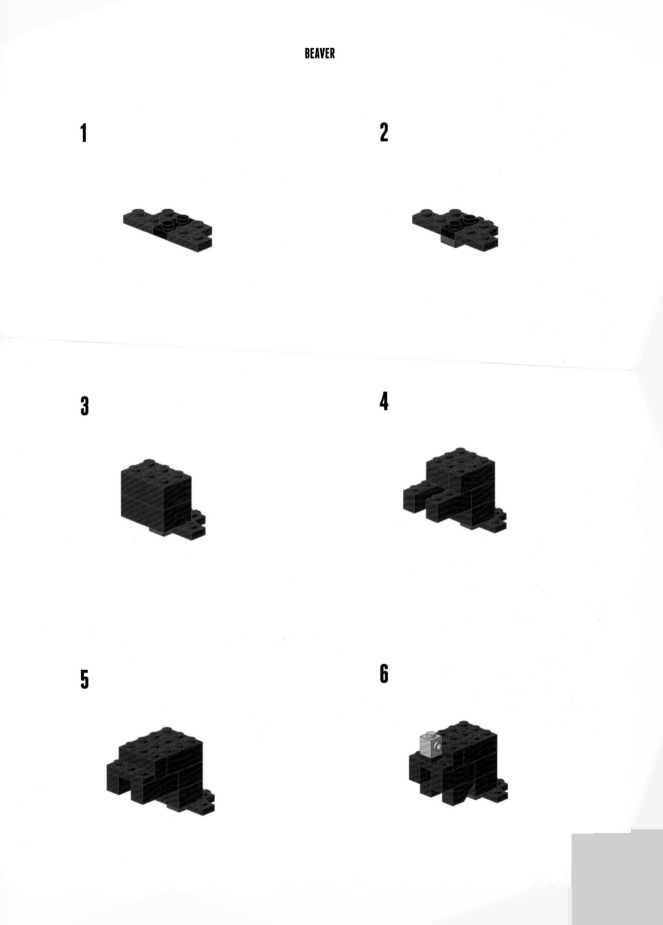

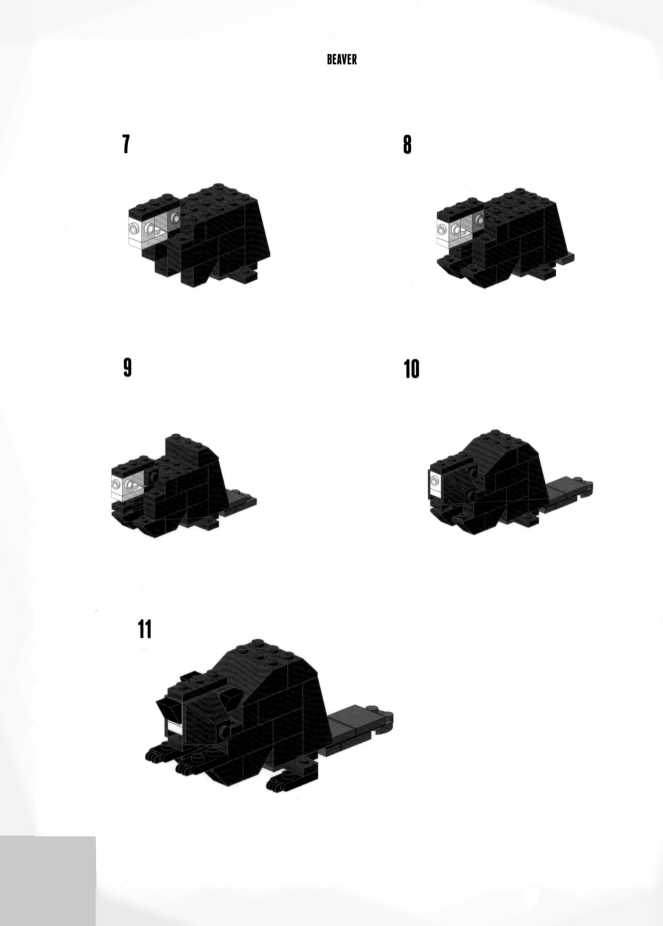

7

8

9

10

11

antelope

Antelopes are grazing animals, closely related to cows, sheep and goats. The males have hollow horns, ranging from short spikes to long corkscrews, and they spend most of their days chewing the cud. Antelopes that live on the plains tend to be larger and slightly slower-moving than those living in more enclosed habitats. The latter are built to bound away quickly if a predator appears!

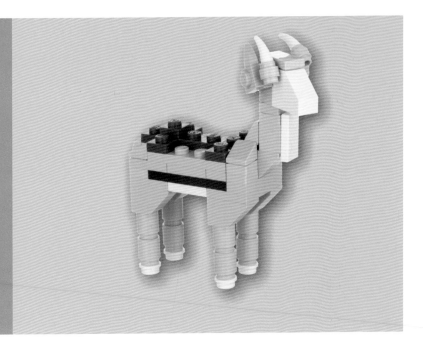

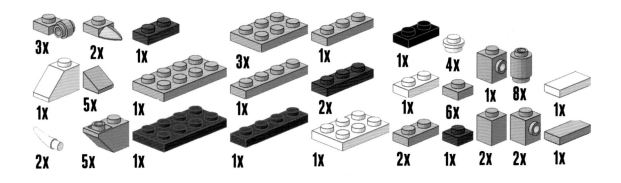

3x 2x 1x 3x 1x 1x 4x

1x 5x 1x 1x 2x 1x 6x 1x 8x 1x

2x 5x 1x 1x 1x 2x 1x 2x 2x 1x

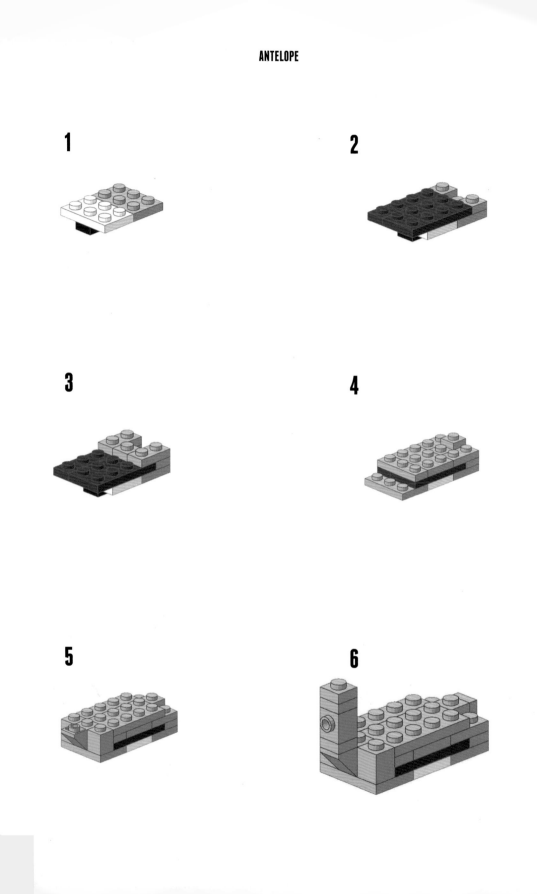

7

8

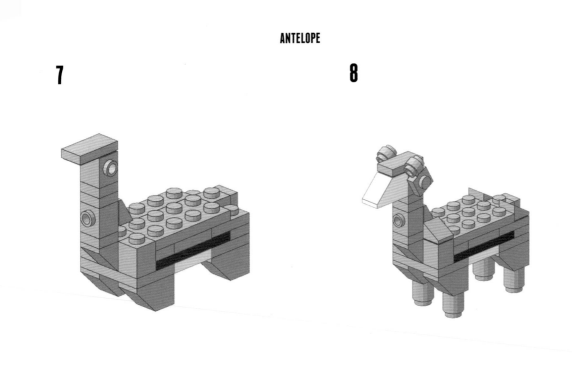

9

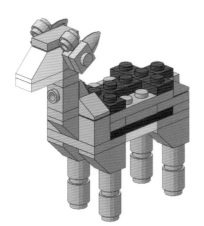

10

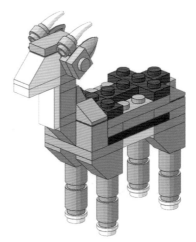

warthog

The warthog is a member of the pig family, found in Africa. They get their name from the two pairs of bumps – or warts – on their faces. They are vegetarians; the tusks on their upper and lower jaws are used for defence. They have a long, thin tail with a tuft at the end. A combination of 1 × 1 headlight bricks, 1 × 1 tiles-with-clip, and horn pieces make up our warthog's snout and tusks. Its ears and hooves are made with 1 × 2 plate-with-tooth and 1 × 1 round plates.

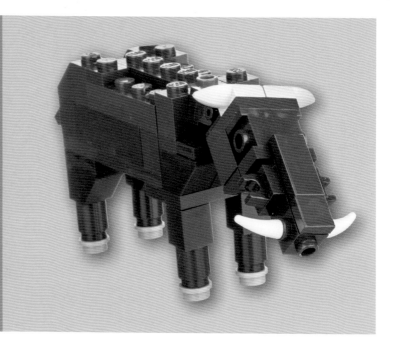

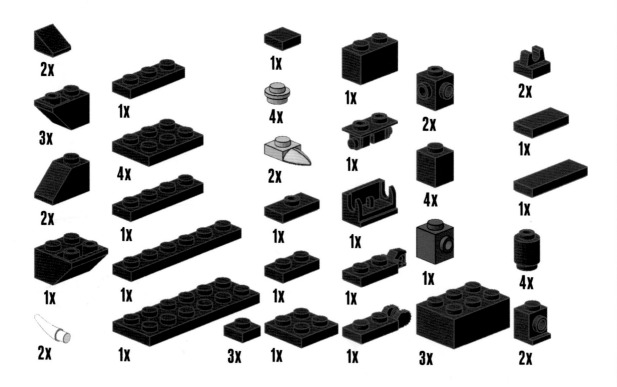

2x

3x

2x

1x

2x

1x

4x

1x

1x

1x

1x

1x

3x

1x

1x

4x

2x

1x

1x

1x

1x

2x

1x

4x

1x

3x

1x

1x

2x

4x

2x

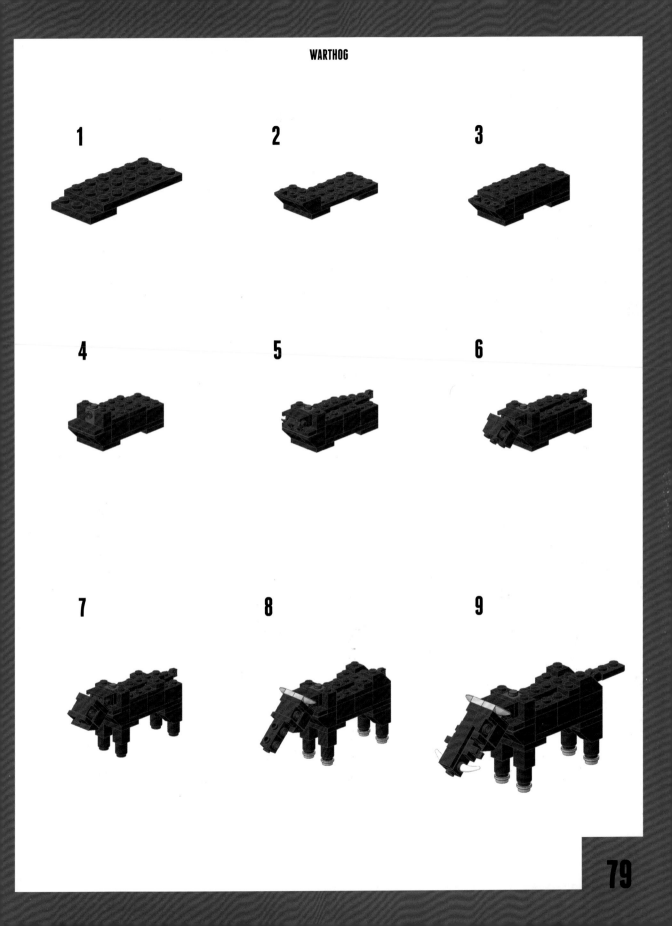

mouse

Eek! Despite being so small, the mouse is feared by many, who dread finding them scurrying around their homes, eating their food! Mice have long, almost hairless tails, big ears, tapered noses and small, sharp claws. We've used a 2 × 2 × 3 cone for our mouse's tapered nose and topped it off with a 1 × 1 round tile in pink. 3 × 3 inverted dishes with 2 × 2 round plates inside serve as ears. A series of 1 × 2, 45-degree slopes create the body shape.

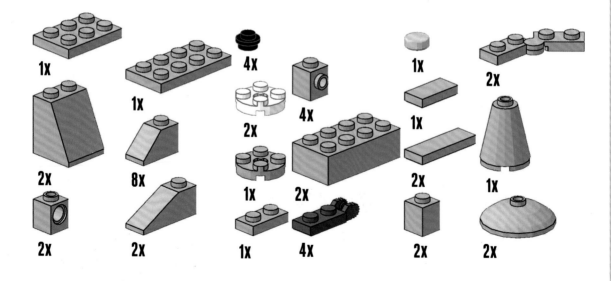

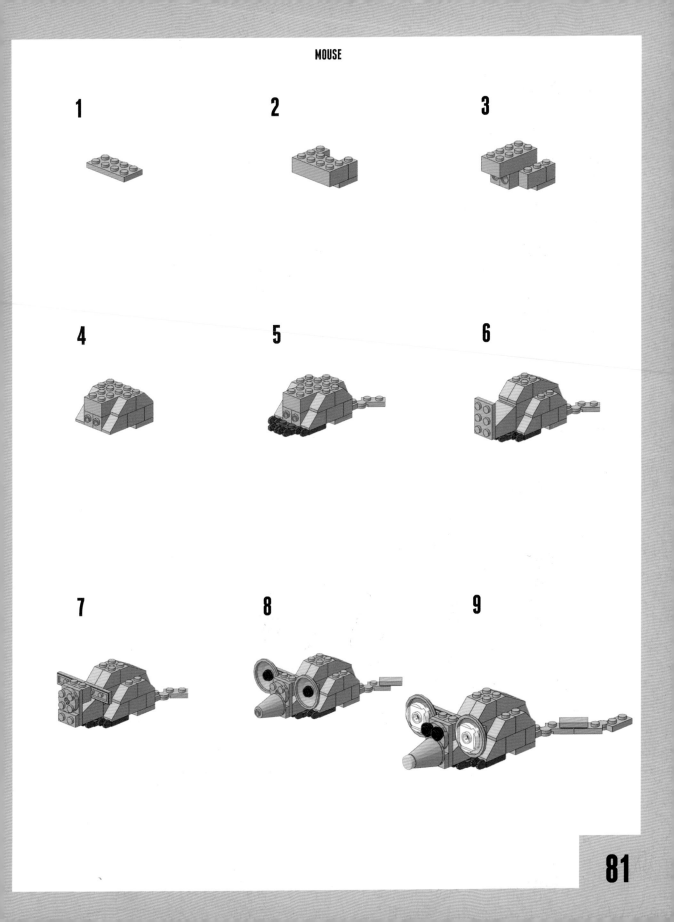

spider

There are more than 43,000 known species of spiders — a creature feared by many people. They have eight legs, and their bodies are divided into two sections. Some spiders actively hunt their prey; they tend to have highly developed senses of touch or sight. We have used 1 x 4 plates-with-hinge to give a great angle for the four pairs of jointed legs. We have recreated the eyes using a 1 x 2 plate-with-angled-bars and 1 x 1 round tiles.

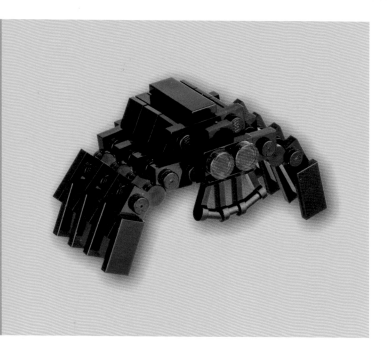

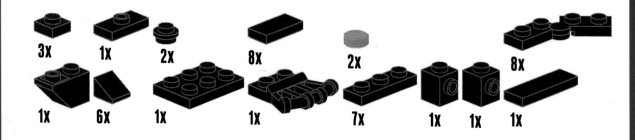

3x   1x   2x   8x   2x   8x

1x   6x   1x   1x   7x   1x   1x   1x

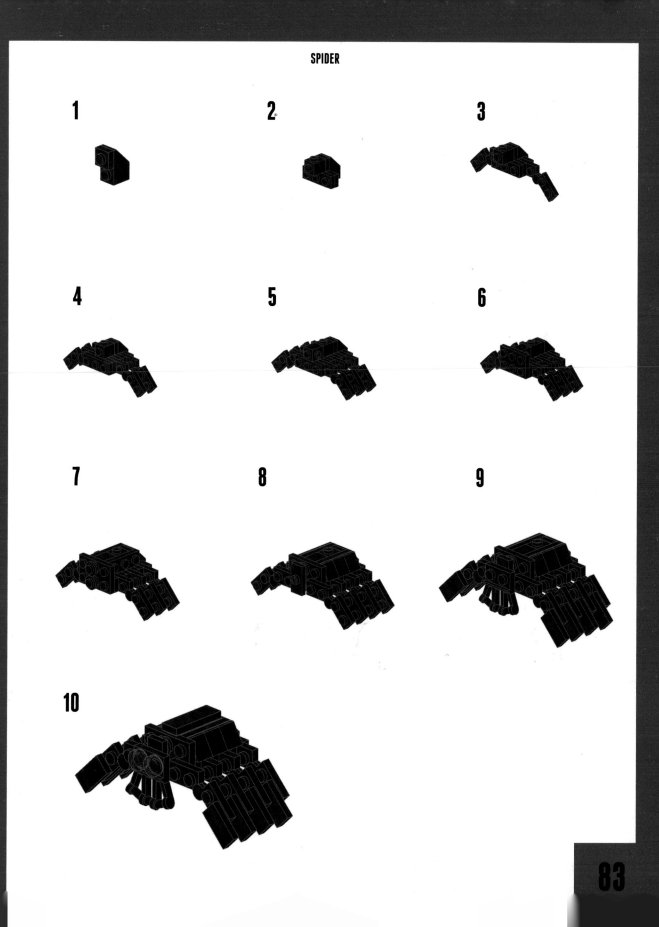

ant

Ants are sociable little creatures; they live together in colonies with organized roles and structures. There are more than 10,000 species of them, and, although they are more common in hot climates, they live all over the world. Ants have a tiny waist that connects their oval abdomen to their thorax – where all three pairs of legs are attached. We've used a mixture of slopes to connect the bulbous thorax and abdomen to the waist.

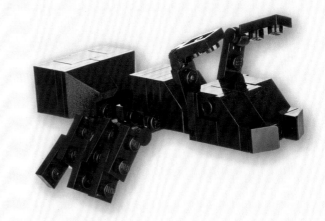

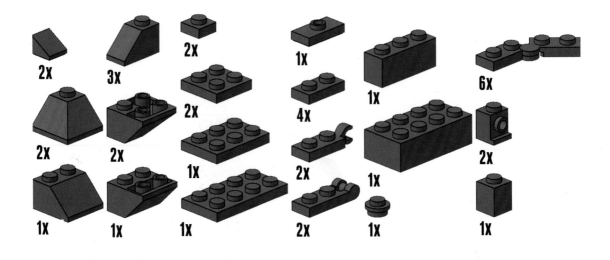

2x 3x 2x 1x 6x

2x 2x 2x 4x 1x 2x

1x 1x 1x 2x 1x 1x

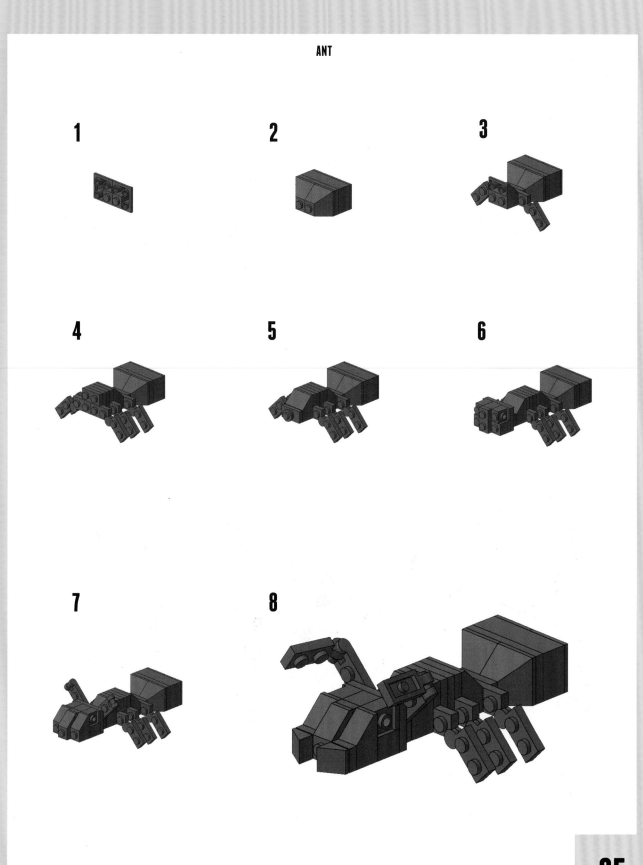

1

2

3

4

5

6

7

8

gorilla

Gorillas are the largest members of the ape family and, except for chimpanzees, are the closest living animals relative to humans. Gorillas are very powerful animals, with black hair and skin, large nostrils, and very obvious brow ridges above their eyes. We're using 2 x 2, 72-degree slopes, mounted upside down to create our silverback gorilla's powerful arms, and small, pale grey slopes for its hands. We've used highlights of pale grey to give it the proverbial silver back.

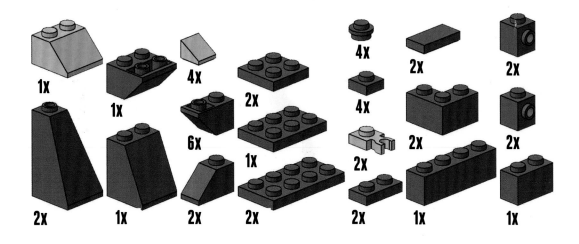

1x

4x

4x

2x

2x

1x

6x

2x

4x

2x

2x

2x

1x

2x

2x

2x

1x

2x

1x

2x

2x

2x

1x

1x

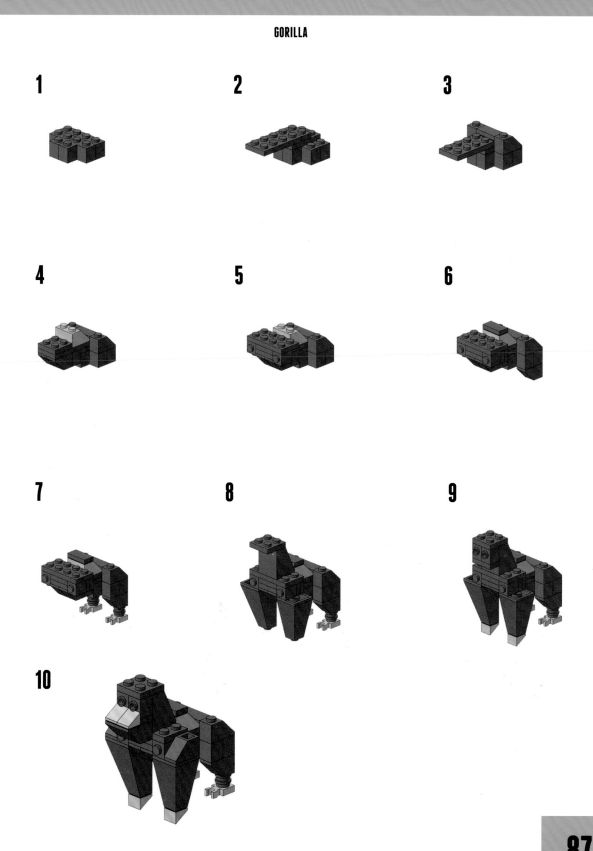

rhinoceros

The rhinoceros is one of the world's largest living land mammals. All species are sadly endangered and are now only found in eastern and southern Africa and some parts of Asia. We've used 2 × 3, 33-degree slopes to replicate the angle of the shoulders and haunches, and a 3 × 3 double-convex 33-degree slope to show the tapering of the body. A large white claw piece gives us the perfect shape for its horn.

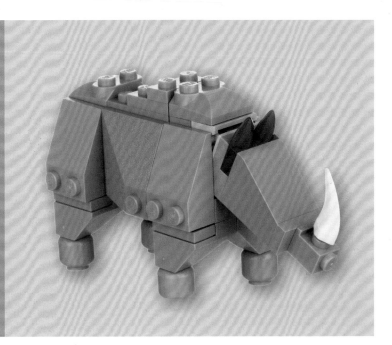

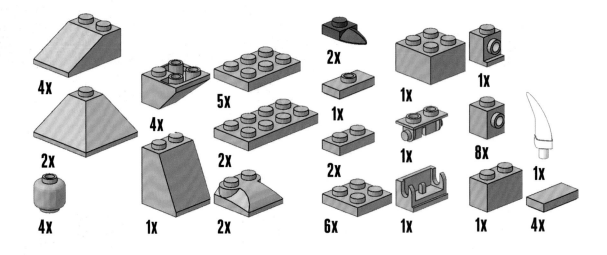

4x

2x

4x

4x

5x

4x

1x

2x

2x

2x

1x

6x

2x

1x

1x

1x

1x

8x

1x

1x

4x

1

2

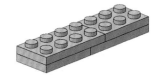

3

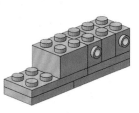

4

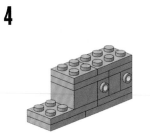

5

6

7

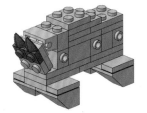

8

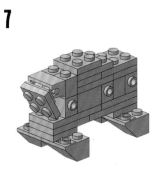

9

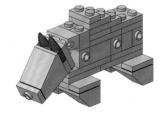

10

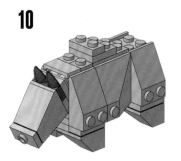

11

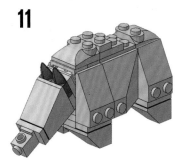

12

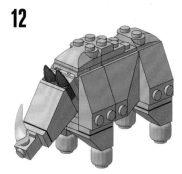

flamingo

Flamingos are bright pink wading birds. They feed with their heads upside down and bills below water, using their webbed feet to stir up the silt, which they filter through their noses to sieve out the algae and tiny crustaceans. Ours is made from small 1-wide pink plates. The head is topped by a 1 × 1 round tile, and the white neck and lower head is made from a drinking glass.

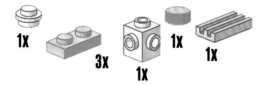

1x   3x   1x   1x   1x

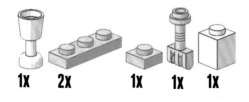

1x   2x   1x   1x   1x

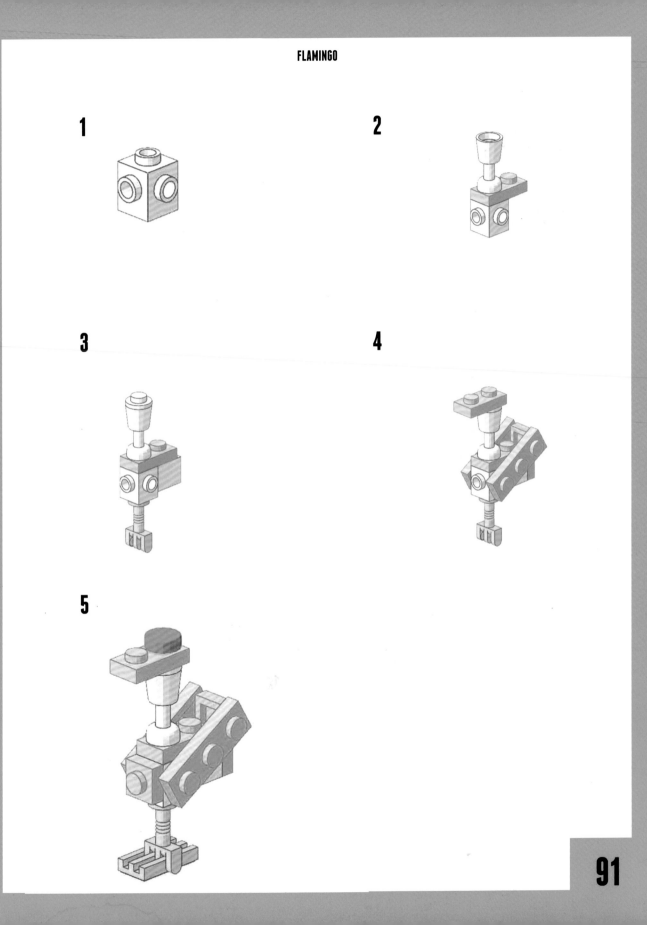

mosquito

Mosquitos are small, midge-like creatures that live off the blood of other animals – including humans! They have a long snout so they can reach blood vessels when they bite. Responsible for transmitting disease, the mosquito is the planet's biggest killer. Here, the legs are made from 1 x 4 antennae, with 1 x 1 cones as knees. Its snout is a 1 x 4 antennae, while its head is made from 3 x 3 inverted dishes and its wings from a 1 x 4 transparent plate.

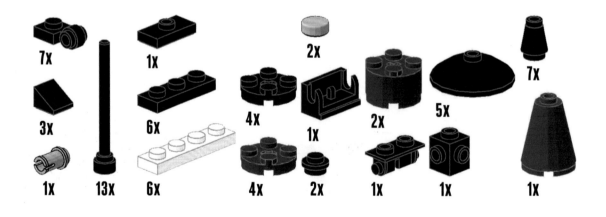

7x

1x

2x

3x

6x

4x

1x

2x

5x

7x

1x

13x

6x

4x

2x

1x

1x

1x

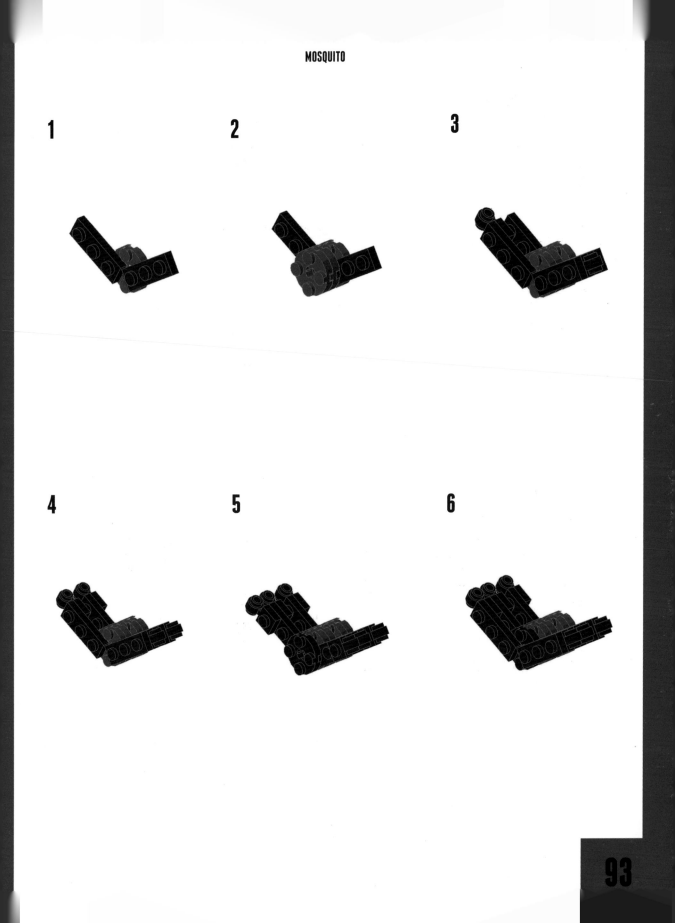

1

2

3

4

5

6

7

8

9

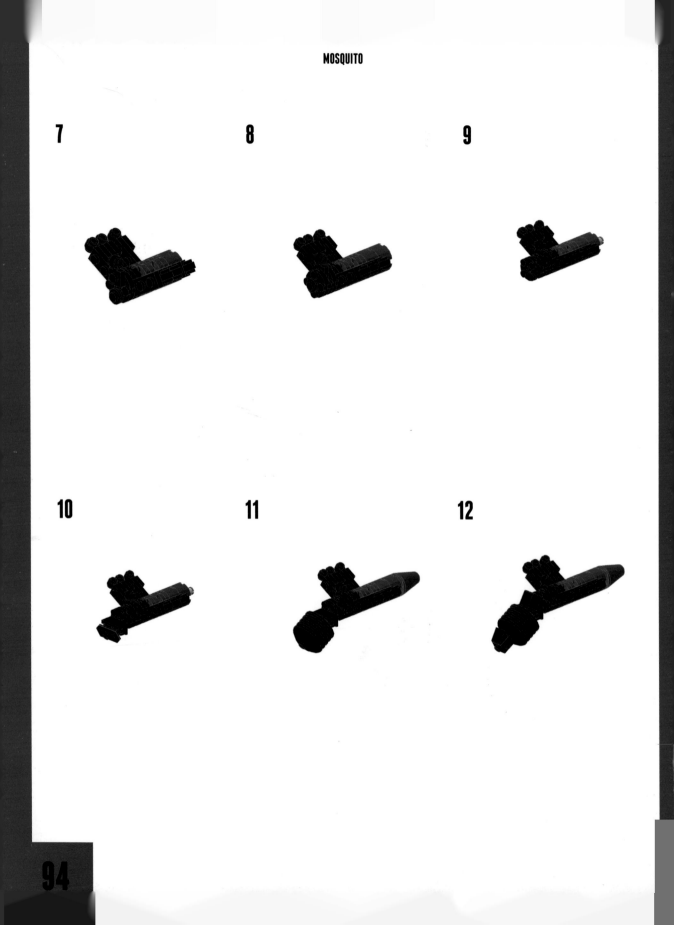

10

11

12

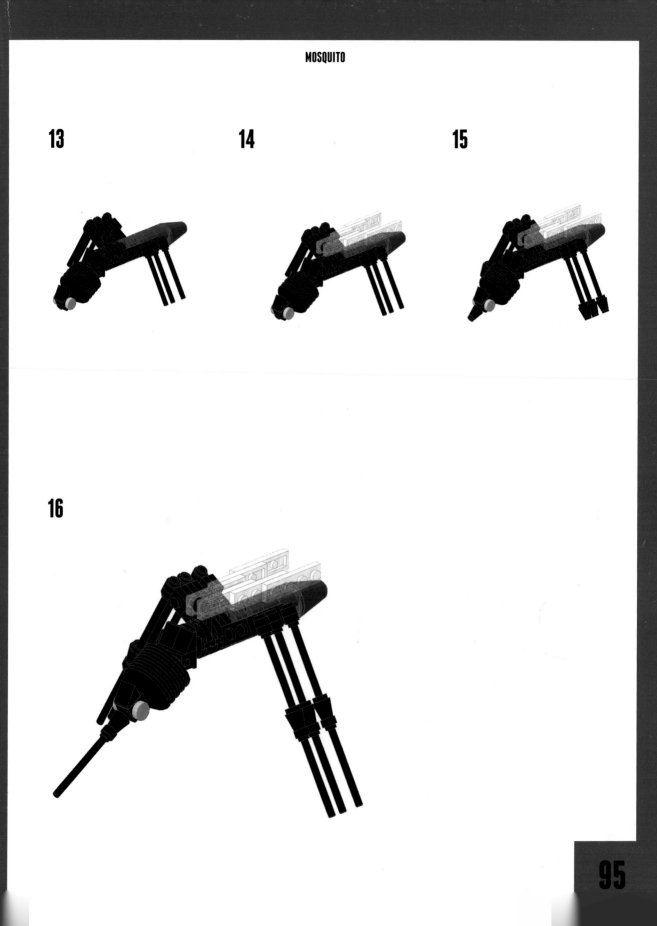

credits

Warren Elsmore, based in Edinburgh, UK, is an artist in LEGO® bricks and a lifelong fan of them. He has been in love with the little plastic bricks since the age of four and now spends his days creating amazing models. After 15 years in a successful IT career, in 2012 Warren moved to working full time with LEGO bricks. He now helps multi-national companies to realize their own dreams in plastic. Warren's best-selling first book, *Brick City*, was released in 21 languages to widespread critical acclaim, and has been followed by a range of books recreating famous places, objects and historical events in LEGO. His models have attracted great press coverage – in fact, thanks to the British Antarctic Survey, one of his models has even made it as far as the South Pole! Exhibitions of Warren's *Brick City* and *Brick Wonders* have toured museums and galleries throughout the United Kingdom, entertaining hundreds of thousands of people. In 2015, Warren co-launched BRICK – the largest LEGO fan event in the United Kingdom, and one of the largest in the world. For more information, visit *warrenelsmore.com*.

Teresa 'Kitty' Elsmore, who researched and co-wrote this book, was a LEGO fan as a child and continues to enjoy creating models today. She is passionate about including all the little details that

bring a scene to life. Since their marriage in 2005, Teresa and Warren have collaborated on a number of projects and now run a successful business together getting paid to make models from LEGO.

Guy Bagley always enjoyed model making as a hobby, but it became his career after he earned an industrial model-making degree at the University of Hertfordshire, UK. After a short spell in the film and TV industry, Guy moved into architectural model making, and finally to toy design with companies such as Mattel and Hasbro. Guy moved to the LEGO group in 1992, where he was involved in planning and building LEGOLAND® Windsor. Next, he became Lead Designer and Model Shop Manager working on new LEGOLAND Theme Parks and LEGOLAND Discovery Centers around the globe. After 23 years he is now pursuing new challenges with Warren Elsmore's team, and has never looked back!

Alastair Disley is a professional LEGO builder, architectural historian and musician. Previously a university lecturer, he lives in the Scottish Borders, UK, with his young family.